THE CONNECTED FATHER

THE CONNECTED FATHER

UNDERSTANDING YOUR UNIQUE ROLE AND RESPONSIBILITIES DURING YOUR CHILD'S ADOLESCENCE

Carl E. Pickhardt, Ph.D.

First published in 2007 by
PALGRAVE MACMILLAN™
175 Fifth Avenue, New York, N.Y. 10010 and
Houndmills, Basingstoke, Hampshire, England RG21 6XS.
Companies and representatives throughout the world.

PALGRAVE MACMILLAN is the global academic imprint of the Palgrave
Macmillan division of St. Martin's Press, LLC and of Palgrave Macmillan
Ltd. Macmillan® is a registered trademark in the United States, United
Kingdom and other countries. Palgrave is a registered trademark in the
European Union and other countries.

ISBN-13: 978-1-4039-7904-9
ISBN-10: 1-4039-7904-9

Library of Congress Cataloging-in-Publication Data is available from the
Library of Congress.

A catalogue record of the book is available from the British Library.

Design by Letra Libre.

First edition: May 2007
10 9 8 7 6 5 4 3 2 1
Printed in the United States of America.

All quotations and case examples used in this book are fictional, made up
by the author to illustrate psychological points. Any resemblance to real
people or situations is coincidental.

*To all those fathers who despair their
teenagers will never grow up,*

and to all those teenagers who prove them wrong.

CONTENTS

PREFACE

This is a "to do" book. It attempts to answer the question: "What are some actions a father can take and words he can say to stay connected to his children during the normal challenges and changes of adolescence?" It discusses a father's "job," a father's "work," a father's "role" as parent and family man. Through numerous explanations, examples, and dialogues, it describes many ways a father can maintain a helpful presence during the ups and downs of the adolescent passage, that period of growth that begins when our sons and daughters start their trial and error journey toward adult independence.

While reading, please keep four provisos in mind.

- First, understand that no father could take every salient stand described in this book. Not only are there too many, but they won't all fit every family situation. Select those ideas and pieces of advice that work for you.
- Second, there are many more ways to stay involved with your teenagers than I describe in this book. My examples are only meant to help you consider a range of fathering choices.
- Third, the gender differences between a father and a mother I describe reflect tendencies, not certainties, with plenty of room for gradations and exceptions.
- And fourth, remember that there is no single definition of fatherhood that fits every father, nor should there be. Past experience, personal makeup, cultural diversity, family traditions, life circumstance, religious training, human nature of the father and the baby, and marital partnership all contribute to the reality that no two fathers define and discharge their role in exactly

the same way. In addition, there are too many positive facets to fatherhood for any man to encompass them all. There is no universal father. A man's job is simply to make a full faith effort within what his human limitations, personal inclinations, and family circumstances allow.

By his individual example, by how he treats his family, by how he conducts himself out in the world, a father has enormous influence on the development of his children, particularly during adolescence, when young people are searching for models with which to identify and to follow. For a father to become *uninvolved* during this critical period is to give up this opportunity, to forsake this influence, and to abandon this responsibility.

This book is *not* about how to be a perfect father. There is no such person. The best any father, like any parent, can give is a human mix of strength and frailty, of good judgment and bad, of consideration and selfishness, of doing right and doing wrong. That's how it is. My goal is *not* to tell you *how* to father but to get you to *think* about what manner of father you want to be, specifically during your children's adolescence, when the hard part of parenting begins.

CHAPTER ONE

CRITICAL DISTINCTIONS FOR READERS TO UNDERSTAND

A FATHER IS NOT A MOTHER, AN ADOLESCENT IS NOT A CHILD

Fatherhood is a threshold moment. Cross that entrance and you not only step from one role into another, but you must also *step up* from being a marriage partner to accepting a daunting array of new responsibilities that redefine your manhood as a nurturer and provider, as parent and family man.

For some men, this challenge of "stepping up" is much more inviting and familiar than for others. Perhaps you can look back at the fathering and family experience you received in a generally positive way, seeing it as an encouraging example to follow. "I want to be as good a dad to my kids as my dad was to me." On the other hand, if you grew up without positive fathering, with emotionally distant or physically absent fathering, or with destructive fathering in an abusive family situation, you may feel frightened by a role that you have no confidence or conception how to fill. At worst, you can feel destined to reenact in a new family setting the old agonies and chaos you knew as a child.

If most of your parenting memories are painful, fatherhood can be a huge and anxiety-provoking adjustment. So rather than engaging with the role, you may take flight and avoid it by leaving the parenting to your wife, by not connecting with your children from the start. You may believe, "I don't know anything about how to father!" Not so. All fathers, like all mothers, give children *two* parental models, not one: how to be and how *not* to be. Where fathers who came out of a positive fathering background can base definitions of their role on "how to be," fathers from a negative fathering background can partly base definitions on "how not to be." They can honestly say to themselves: "I know a lot about fathering from being shown how *not* to behave." And from that negative beginning an affirmative alternative can be built: "Based on that experience, what kind of father do I want to be?" a dad can ask. Then helpful answers will come to mind. "I can be appreciative, and not dissatisfied. I can be encouraging, and not critical. I can be interested, and not dismissive. I can be accessible, and not too busy. I can listen in disagreement, and not shut communication down. I can remain safe and reasonable in conflict, and not become threateningly explosive."

You are not destined to repeat past unhappiness *if* you commit to profit from the negative example you were so painfully given. In counseling, I see fathers free themselves from what they knew to create what they want.

A FATHER IS NOT A MOTHER

In the process of contrasting the fathering you received and the fathering you want to provide, you also have to make another distinction: *A father is not a mother.* This biological difference shapes the development of parental roles, and your role as father, from the beginning.

After your child's birth, you have a lot of parental catching up to do because father and mother begin their separate relationships with the baby at completely different times and places. Through nine months of pregnancy, the labor of birthing, and the intimacy of breast-feeding, your wife begins a relationship of deep physical attachment; she is closely connected with the child from the outset in mysterious ways you can never experience. She comes to know the baby (and the baby comes to know her) both inside the womb and out.

Your wife starts as part of the child because the child starts as part of her, systemically dependent on her, sharing her blood, inhabiting her body. *In the mother, of the mother, and from the mother* is how connection to the female parent begins. The mother has a bonded relationship with the infant from the start. This is an unfathomable connection to you. Lack of this founding connection, of course, does *not* mean you cannot build deep, strong, abiding attachment to your child. Remember, if adoptive, step, and foster parents who are neither physically bonded nor biologically linked with their children can powerfully connect; an attentive and involved biological father can certainly attach as well. As Brott (1997) notes in his book *The New Father,* "Although the vast majority of research on attachment has focused on mothers and children, some researchers are now beginning to study father-child attachment. Their findings confirm what active, involved fathers have known in their hearts for years—that the father-child bond is no less important than the mother-child bond."

Both presence and absence of early bonding can influence the later development of the parental role. A mother literally sacrifices her body for the baby, who parasitically depends on her for protection, sustenance, and life. While she is pregnant, the father supports the baby by supporting the mother. Often these early commitments portend how mother and father will differentiate their respective parental gender roles later on. A mother may become the more sacrificial parent, inclined to set her self-interest and well-being aside for the child's care, while the father may become the more practically supportive parent, inclined to invest himself in home improvement and at the job for the sake of family. This distinction is a tendency, not a certainty, since a mother can certainly support a family and a father can certainly sacrifice as a parent.

Contrasted to your wife, you begin your relationship with the baby at a distance. Although your newborn immediately recognizes her, at the outset you are a stranger. Even if you assisted at the birth, you must earn the infant's attachment after delivery is over by physically and emotionally, non-verbally and verbally, creating a presence in the baby's family world, creating a bond the baby can come to trust and love and rely on over time.

Although attachment between mother and child is present from the start, for fathers it takes positively perceived performance (tending, touching, and talking) for the infant to develop attachment. Likewise, the child soon learns to perform in positively perceived ways to earn your approval. Pleasing each other has a lot to do with how the father/infant connection is forged. *Between father and child, approval mediates attachment.* While the mother/child connection tends to feel more unconditional because it is physically inherent, connection between you and your child can feel more conditional because, through performance, approval must be earned.

Interestingly enough, this is a distinction commonly heard during the teenage years. "Mom worries about how I am; Dad's more concerned with how I do." During adolescence, when teenage separation and differentiation put stress on the teen's relationship with parents, the founding distinction between the acceptance-based mother and the approval-based father can gain currency again.

We can see this difference in action with a late adolescent in counseling who is planning to introduce a serious love interest to his parents. "I want my mom to *like* who I bring home, and my dad to *approve.*" Or a young adolescent who states: "I want my mom to love me and I want to make my dad proud." This distinction is very important for you as a father to keep in mind during your children's adolescence. Your disapproval of their performance at critical junctures in their growth can disconnect you and your teenagers when they need your presence for security, stability, and support.

Consider two different fathering responses to a teenager's misadventure. "After you pulling a dumb stunt like this, I wonder if you'll ever learn!" or "I'll keep you company while you deal with the consequences of what you did." If you were the teenager, which response would you like to receive? As the father, which response would you want to give? *When it comes to staying connected to—or becoming disconnected from—your adolescent, as a father you must be sensitive to how you manage your evaluative power.*

The old parenting advice is still good: Disapprove of the behavior, but never the person. "Just because I disagree with your choice doesn't mean I love you any less for what you did." Your parental approval needs to be kept separate from, and subordinated to, your acceptance. While approval gives affirmation of actions, acceptance assumes innate value and worth. As a father, you need to clearly communicate that your acceptance is constant and unconditional, while your approval is conditional on conduct, rising or falling depending on choices your teenager makes. Your acceptance does not guarantee your approval ("Part of my job is to let you know how I think you're doing"), but your disapproval will not alter the guarantee of your acceptance ("No matter how you do, your loving standing with me is secure").

I believe the early infant bonding difference between mother and father can contribute to later gender differences in parental roles. However, the interaction of sex, gender, and parental roles remains complex, part of the unresolved and ongoing debate in professional psychology about sexual differences and the operating differences they create (see Rhoads, 2005.)

My perspective is that both sexual nature and nurture play a part in differentiating maternal and paternal roles. Biologically, fathers do not start parenthood with the history of physical attachment to the infant and early bonding that mothers do, while men and women learn different gender definitions growing up. As will be more fully described, the social sex role-training boys and girls tend to receive in same-sex peer groups commonly diverges, male growth often focused more on competition and competency, female growth often focused more on communication and intimacy. As a consequence, I have come to believe that men typically bring more of a performance emphasis to fatherhood and women typically bring a more relational emphasis to motherhood.

This greater sensitivity can serve a mother well from the onset of the child-parent relationship because insight can increase attachment. "Mothers classified as positively insightful were rated as more sensitive and were more likely to have securely attached children than were mothers not classified as positively insightful." (See Koren-Karie, Oppenheim, Sher, and Etzion-Carasso in *Developmental Psychology*, vol. 38, no. 4, July 2002.) During infancy, a mother's instincts about what the baby needs or about what might be wrong are usually more sensitive than a father's due to the greater depth of attachment she brings to parenting, and it is to that greater sensitivity that the infant responds. The man needs more time to "feel" and "read" the baby's non-verbal language of pleasure and distress in order to understand the personality and temperament of this little stranger born into his care.

I have often been struck by how mothers are often more sensitive to emotional undercurrents in their teenagers, more observant of subtle trouble signs, than are fathers, who tend to focus on obvious behaviors and major indicators of difficulty. So instead of treating what your wife says as unjustified concern over unidentifiable causes, it generally behooves you to credit the keener emotional sensitivity and insight she may provide. Rather than criticize, "You worry too much," you might be wise to ask, "What do you sense might be going wrong?" My experience in counseling is that most fathers are simply not as sensitively tuned in to their teenagers as mothers are.

Here is an example. A mother senses something amiss, even dangerous, about her daughter's date, though there's no evidence so support her suspicion. So she confides to her husband, "Something about that young man she is going out with tonight doesn't feel right to me. I can't tell you exactly what." Rather than discounting his wife's response as "groundless worry," he looks more closely himself and encourages his wife to share her unease with their daughter, which the woman does. "I don't have specific cause for concern to base this on, but I want you to know that for whatever reason I'm not feeling entirely comfortable with your date tonight, so I'd like you to be more watchful than usual when you go out." Later, the daughter uses the mother's discomfort to support her own. When the guy suggests going to a party after the movie, she decides to come directly home instead. As a psychologist, I've seen the protective value of mysterious maternal knowing many times.

Of course, the power of maternal attachment, like most human traits, is double-edged, creating strengths on the one hand and problems on the other. Because mother and baby begin so closely attached, the hard growth issues later on in adolescence often have to do with creating adequate separation. So the teenage son complains to his mother: "You're overprotective, you need to let me go!" Because father and baby begin so separated, the hard growth issues in adolescence often have to do with creating and maintaining adequate attachment.

So the teenager daughter complains to her father: "What do you care, you don't even know me!"

Because many fathers have been socialized to base relationships on companionship and on doing activities together, attaching to an infant can be a challenge. While mothers can increase sensitivity and sense of connection by simply watching an infant, many fathers are often less observant and patient watchers because there is no action to take. Often waiting several years until they and their children can start "doing things together," these men don't start to build significant attachment until the child is older and more capable of interactive play, which is sometimes sexually differentiated, rougher with a son, more gentle with a daughter.

The child's bond to the father, however, is always different from that to the mother, a difference that should be respected and accepted to this degree: *It is not the father's job to copy or compete for the maternal role, to imitate or try to be an extra mother.* His job is to *complement* her role by providing a significant, additional parental presence in his own personally distinctive way.

Of course, a father can do many "mothering" acts his spouse does. Apart from breastfeeding, a father can fully participate in the complete range of childcare. He can also express those traditionally "feminine" traits of nurturing, empathy, sensitivity, and comfort. He usually cannot, however, make up right away for the parental role training in family care-giving that girls tend to practice more than boys do growing up.

Fathering situations where these traits tend to be well expressed are in families in which the same-sex couple is male. Gay fathers can be much less inhibited than straight fathers about expressing their sensitive, vulnerable, empathetic side, thereby encouraging that emotional expression and connection with their teenagers. "Gay fathers appear to be particularly interested in extending their masculine identity to embrace nurturing qualities." (See Dunne, *The Journal of Sexualities,* vol. 4, no. 2, May 2001.)

Growing up, men and women are socialized to fit different sex roles, and they bring those differences into their respective roles as fathers and mothers. As children in same-sex peer groups, they find the continuum of characteristics available to all human beings divided into separate sexual camps. "Masculine" and "feminine" are defined exclusively, to a degree that dehumanizes young people, who feel forced to fit simplified gender distinctions that are developmentally sexist in their restrictive ways. Cross over that divide, and as a girl exhibit "masculine" traits or interests (like fighting physically), or as a boy exhibit "feminine" traits or interests (like playing with dolls), and cruel teasing for appearing unwomanly or unmanly was likely to follow.

How you were socialized to define your manhood growing up is a large part of the sex role definition you bring to fathering. While sexual differences are endowed, gender differences are learned through such influences as cultural ideals, parental identification, social instructions, and peer interactions. For example, socialization may explain why and when many young adolescent girls can be socially discouraged from acting extremely angry ("male" behavior) and many young adolescent boys can be socially encouraged not to cry ("female" behavior). So reading strong emotion at this age can be confusing when girls, feeling extremely angry, express it in tears, and boys, feeling badly hurt, express it in anger.

Sex role education also may explain why male and female teenagers can be prone to despondency from different gender-related causes, performance failures more often depressing to young men, relationship failures more often depressing to young women. For many adolescent boys, performance is the major pillar of self-esteem and source of identity ("I am how I do"), and for many adolescent girls, relationship is the major pillar of self-esteem and source of identity ("I am who my friends are"). Studies have documented this difference. "The interpersonal depressive style more frequent for girls than boys, and characterized by helplessness and fear of abandonment by others, was compared with the self-criticism depressive style, characterized by preoccupation about feelings of competency and loss of self-esteem" in boys. (See Marcotte, Alain, and Gosselin, in *Sex Roles: A Journal of Research,* July 1999.)

No wonder women tend to sacrifice performance for the sake of relationships and men tend to sacrifice relationships for the sake of performance. They were trained to think that way. Just like women tend to seek support when adversity strikes, and men tend to go it alone.

In early adolescence (ages 9–13), both sexes begin to mask their own sexual insecurity by labeling boys who appear insufficiently masculine and girls who appear insufficiently feminine as "gay." This is consequently a time when young people who are beginning to come to honest terms with their homosexuality go into lonely hiding. And it is when parents, if they so choose, can weigh in against this fearful and hostile teasing so their children learn to accept and respect the normal range of sexual variation.

At this early adolescent stage, early adolescent girls are under more pressure to look and act feminine and boys are under more pressure to look and act masculine, as both imitate sexual ideals in the popular culture. Both are now increasingly preoccupied with appearance, with acting and looking "sexy"—extremely womanly or manly in physically compelling, socially prescribed ways that are portrayed by young models and icons celebrated in the popular media. Look at the later adolescent years at high school, for example at football games, and you will find young women cheerleaders and dancers in formfitting costumes dressed to play the role of female attractor, to motivate and to entertain. At the same event, young men, bulked up in padding, are dressed to play the role of male aggressor in a collision sport.

So much about "male" and "female" gender distinctions is socially and culturally made. Thus your manhood as a father is powerfully formed in your boyhood. Not only does your childhood experience shape your own beliefs about masculine and feminine, but it sets gender expectations you bring to male and female children who, come adolescence, start experimenting with what it means to become young men and young women. It is worth taking time to clarify your own sex role definitions, since they will influence your responses to how your teenage son and daughter start to grow. It may be hard for you to remember that adolescents are not in this world to fulfill your gender expectations. They are responsible for finding and defining their own. Your responsibility is to understand and accept what those are. For example, just as a socially outgoing wife must learn to appreciate her more shy and private daughter, a former high school jock and current sports enthusiast must learn to appreciate his non-athletic, artistic son.

In addition to differences in gender definitions of male and female, there are also differences in how male and female are socialized in same-sex relationships to form friendships. "Studies examining gender differences in adolescent reports of intimacy indicate that females (1) develop more intimate friendships, (2) stress the importance of maintaining intimacy, and (3) expect more intimacy in their friendships than do males." (See Johnson in *Adolescence,* summer 2004.)

Young women tend to rely more on talking together, confiding in each other, and sharing emotional experiences and inner thoughts to create intimacy, while young men tend to rely more on doing activities together, such as games and sports, and engaging in adventures to create companionship. Young women tend to establish closeness through giving support and personal disclosure, and often draw primary self-esteem from the power of relationships; how they are *feeling* becomes a reliable measure of how well things are going. Young men, however, tend to establish closeness through sharing exploits and competition, and often draw primary self-esteem from the power of performance; how they are *doing* becomes a reliable measure of how well things are going. From this early training among same-sex peers, girls are often socialized to be more emotionally sensitive, empathetic, and to talk out feelings, and boys to be more emotionally suppressed, to tough it up, and to act feelings out.

Because of how they are socialized differently with male peers growing up, men often become the performance-focused parent, encouraging activity and achievement (pushing for success), while women, socialized with female peers growing up, often become the relationally focused parent, encouraging communication and support (valuing affiliation). Sometimes, teenagers will observe this distinction when describing their relationships with their parents: "I do more things with my dad, but I talk about more stuff with my mom." On balance, the father is often more of the "how are you doing?" performance parent, and the mother is often more of the "how are you feeling?" empathetic parent. "Dad coaches me, and mom listens to me."

Come adolescence, this female (relationship-focused) and male (performance-focused) distinction can also have a bearing on the predominant kind of emotional pain that adolescents frequently report experiencing with their parents. Because the mother is the more relationally focused and sacrificial parent, blame over failed obligation to her can inspire guilt in the teenager: "I don't honor my mother enough for all she does for me," "I don't treat my mother as well as she deserves." Because the father is the more achievement focused and evaluative parent, blame over failed performance can inspire shame in the teenager: "I'm not turning out as well as my father wants," "I'm disappointing my father's expectations." It is best for a mother not to guilt a teenager for inadequate appreciation and for a father not to shame a teenager for inadequate performance. In both cases, the pain can run very deep, particularly along same-sex connections where a daughter feels she can't do enough for her mom, and a son feels he can't do well enough for his dad.

None of the foregoing is to say a father cannot be a well-connected and committed parent, only that the mother, with her relational strengths, often fills this role. Consider the social evidence about commitment. More fathers abandon children than do mothers, who make up the preponderance of unwed parents heading single-parent homes. After divorce (and not just because of judicial bias), more mothers than fathers undertake day-to-day custodial responsibility. According to "Facts about Single Parent Families," drawn from the 2000 U.S. Census by Parents Without Partners (see ParentsWithoutPartners.org): "One parent families numbered over 12 million in 2000. . . . Of all custodial parents, 85% were mothers and 15% were fathers. . . . About one-third of custodial mothers have never been married."

This is not to say there have not been changes. "According to the U.S. Census Bureau's March 2002 Current Population Survey, among two-parent households, there were 189,000 with stay-at-home dads. Though this figure is small next to the 11 million children living with stay-at-home moms, the number of children living with stay-at-home dads has risen 18% since 1994." (See Dunham, *The Wall Street Journal Online,* 09/02/2003.)

However, even with more equitable sharing in divorce custody than there used to be, even with more fathers heading single-parent families, even with more stay-at-home dads, even with more fathers more involved in the family than their fathers were, the vast preponderance of single-parent mothers suggests that more women step up to the challenges and responsibilities of active parenthood than men. *By history of attachment at birth and being socialized to value nurturing relationships, mothers tend to be the more committed parent.*

In the extremes, mothers and fathers can fall prey to different parental shortcomings. A mother, over-committed to relationships, can excessively focus on others at her own expense. She can neglect her own well-being, give away too much attention, take too much responsibility, and end up self-sacrificing to her personal cost. A father, over-committed to his own performance, can excessively focus on himself at others' expense. He can neglect their well-being for his own, become excessively self-preoccupied, demand too much attention, be inadequately considerate, concerned, and responsive, and end up self-centered at the cost of his family. Many mothers would benefit from becoming more self-attentive like their husbands, and many fathers would benefit from becoming more other-attentive like their wives.

THE FATHER AS A PERFORMANCE-FOCUSED PARENT

In sum, because of lack of parental attachment at birth and male socialization growing up, fathers tend to be the *performance parent,* primarily focused on *doing* (actions and conduct), *ability* (interests and mastery), and *well doing* (prowess and success). As a man, a father tends to offer a different emphasis than a mother, who tends to be the *relationship parent,* primarily focused on *being* (experience and emotion), *being connected* (communication and intimacy), and *well-being* (esteem and happiness).

Evolutionary psychology has marshaled an enormous amount of data from studies about developmental sex differences that tends to support this performance focus/relationship focus distinction between men and women, and consequently between fathers and mothers. In his book, *Male, Female: The Evolution of Human Sex Differences* (1998), psychologist David Geary describes how from "the selective imitation of competitive activities, and actual experiences with same-sex peer groups, boys learn to best achieve within-group social dominance and practice the specific competencies associated with male-male competition in their particular culture. They learn how to achieve cultural success." He further describes "the greater attentiveness of girls and women to social cues (e.g., facial expression), their greater social signaling (e.g., smiling), their skill at strategically using emotion cues in social contexts, and their general motivation to develop intimate social relationships as an end in itself."

Obviously, each focus makes a vital contribution to a child's growth. Even more important to keep in mind, the distinction does not mean women are always going to be superior at relating and men are always going to be superior at performing. Evidence from your experience will amply demonstrate that there are many men with highly developed relational skills and many women who are extremely high performers.

However, it is comfort with the performance focus that causes many fathers to find the *coaching role* congenial—a way to combine instruction and motivation to help a son or daughter develop physical competence, discipline from practice, social obedience, team spirit, and competitive drive. Additionally, some non-demonstrative, non-communicative fathers most comfortably express their love by performing on their jobs in reliable ways that help support their families.

Mother as "warm and nurturing," father as "cold and distant" is a distinction that I still frequently hear from parents describing their parents, and from teenagers describing family, portraying the relational woman and the performance man. And yet, on deeper inspection what is often revealed is not that the mother was or is more loving than the father, but that *love is communicated in different ways.* While the mother may tend to directly express love to the child through declaration and affection, the father may tend to demonstrate love through reliable service and work. "My father never told me that he loved me, and unlike my mother he was not one to give hugs. But from all the things he did for me and family he showed his love in a million different ways." Being able to honestly come to this realization can shatter the myth of the uncaring father who never told you he loved you. The danger is that if you do not realize that your father demonstrated love through loyal actions, not loving words, you may feel unloved when you are not. Through his faithful performance in the family, through a host of contributions you relied upon, he *showed* you his love. For many men, perhaps now in an older generation, it is through steadfast job support that they primarily contributed caring to their family. This performance was their primary parental act of love.

From what I have seen in counseling, the besetting sin of the father as performance-focused parent is his misguided belief that dogged disapproval will cause his teenagers to try harder and do better. "I'll keep criticizing you until your attitude and motivation improve!" In fact, excessive criticism only hurts the teenager's feelings and discourages him from wanting to hear what the father has to say and from doing what the father wants him to do. The paternal criticism is offensive, not appreciated. The teen wants less to do with him and for him, not more. And the father contaminates his connection with his teenager by provoking his increased resentment and dislike. "Dad is never satisfied, no matter how I do, which is all he really cares about!" As a performance coach, a father would be far better served by praising the good than by only faulting mistakes in the misguided belief that his expressions of dissatisfaction will cause improvement.

A teenage daughter tends to suffer from her father's unrelenting criticism the worst. His constant censure and lack of positive valuing can gut her sense of self-worth, sending her in search of other men to provide approval, men who may exploit her unmet emotional need for affirmation in a variety of harmful ways. Then when she gets into trouble, all she gets from her father is further blame. *Fathers: Don't get so caught up in control, criticism, and correction that you neglect giving the approval and acceptance your teenagers sorely need.*

Finally, consider the allocation of performance focus and relationship focus in the parental roles that your teenagers perceive in you and their mother, and receive from you both. You may want to keep the mix as it is or you may want to change some of it, but at least you need to be aware of it. After all, what you both give your children is who and how you are.

So to help start your self-evaluation, ask yourself which, if any, of the following statements your teenagers would say hold true for each of you.

- A father tends to talk more about what and how you are *doing* and a mother tends to talk more about what and how you are *feeling*.
- A father tends to value *intelligence* most highly and a mother tends to place more value on *sensitivity*.
- A father tends to be intolerant of *"stupidity"* and a mother tends to be intolerant of *"meanness."*
- A father tends to be more focused on his *job* and a mother tends to be more focused on her *family*.

- A father tends to talk about *working hard,* achieving, and preparing for the future and a mother tends to talk about *having friends,* being supportive, and staying well connected.
- A father tends to want to *stop disagreements* and a mother tends to want to *hear what disagreements have to say.*
- A father tends to be more *evaluative* of what is happening and a mother tends to be more *accepting* of what is happening
- A father tends to *challenge* your opinions and a mother tends to *listen* to your opinions.
- A father tends to do more *outside activities* with children and a mother tends to provide more *care taking* at home.
- A father tends to *argue to win* and a mother tends to *discuss to understand.*
- A father tends to *say too little* and a mother tends to *say too much.*
- A father tends to want to *fix problems right away* and a mother tends to want to *find out what's going on.*
- A father tends to *go for control* and a mother tends to *express concern.*
- A father tends to be *uncomfortable in conflict* and wants to shut it down and a mother tends to be more *patient in conflict,* talking divisive issues out.

These kinds of differences tend to flow from the contrast between performance and relationship focus that fathers and mothers often bring to parenting, differences that are chosen, not fixed, and with practice are susceptible to change. Remember that marriage is a union in which partners can profit from each other. Over time a mother may claim some characteristics valued in her husband that she did not initially possess, and a father may claim some characteristics valued in his wife that he did not initially possess. "Because my husband is a great problem solver, I have learned to become a better problem solver myself." "Because my wife is great at speaking up about uncomfortable issues, I have learned to become better at speaking up myself."

The performance contribution that fathers can make to children is very positive. It just needs to not exclude concerns for the whole person a son and daughter is becoming, particularly during adolescence, when teenagers are redefining and developing themselves across the full range of who and how they are. Hence that common teenage complaint against a father: "All you ever ask me about is how I'm *doing* at school!" Doesn't the dad know that "student" is a very small part of the larger person his teenage son or daughter is becoming? Isn't he interested? Doesn't he care? *Maintain perspective: Treat your adolescent as a person first, and a performer second.*

AN ADOLESCENT IS NOT A CHILD

Because they tend to be the more committed parent and are more comfortable navigating the emotional depths of relationships, more mothers seem to have what it takes to maintain communication, concern, and caring during adolescence, when close and compliant children become more abrasive and unfamiliar to live with. Gone is the little girl or little boy that used to be so easy and such fun to be with. Consider just a few common changes from childhood to adolescence.

- From being close to becoming more distant;
- From being considerate to being self-centered;
- From being adoring of you to being more critical;
- From going to bed early to staying up late and sleeping in;
- From liking what you like to liking what you don't;
- From being positive to being more negative;
- From being disclosing to being more private;
- From being truthful to being more deceptive;
- From being industrious to being more lazy;
- From being compliant to being more resistant;
- From enjoying family to preferring time with friends;
- From being agreeable to being more argumentative;
- From wanting good grades to being more content to just get by.

Now preoccupied with getting more freedom, the adolescent starts contesting rules, delaying compliance, getting more deeply into peer attachments, experiencing the forbidden, setting an independent agenda, and experimenting with new identities.

Faced with these unwelcome but normal adolescent changes, fathers (feeling disappointed) risk becoming critical in response. Faced with normal adolescent disaffection and separation, fathers (feeling rejected) risk pulling away in response. Faced with normal adolescent resistance and argument, fathers (feeling angry) risk going for control, using the threat of punishment to shut disagreement down or force compliance. Criticism, rejection, and anger by the father during this time of painful transition tend to disconnect him from his children, not keep him close.

For many fathers, increased abrasion during adolescence can be particularly trying, especially when comfort with conflict and tolerance for opposition was low to begin with. For these men, adolescence can put their commitment to fathering to the test. Are they going to hang in there, or bow out? Are they going to stay actively involved, or turn parenting over to their wife?

A mother's historical attachment, stronger parental commitment, and determination to remain constantly involved can serve her well during these stormy adolescent times, while a father's historical distance can cause him to become less involved when the adolescent going gets tough. In addition, parenting a teenage son and parenting a teenage daughter will test a father in very different, but very challenging ways. As will be discussed (see chapters 11 and 12), for an adolescent son there will be "measuring up" issues to be addressed and the problems of comparison to his dad. And for an adolescent daughter there will be "respect" issues to be addressed and problems of being taken seriously as a woman by her father.

CHAPTER TWO

WHY FATHERS DISCONNECT FROM ADOLESCENTS

This book is written to help you hang in there as a father and not opt out of active parenting when your children enter adolescence. During this period of high risk, young people need the supportive, salient, and stabilizing presence of a father more than ever to help anchor, structure, and guide healthy teenage growth.

Why would a father "opt out?" In simple terms, because the rewards of parenting diminish as the adolescent becomes less positively responsive, less easy to manage, and less simple to deal with. The parenting usually takes more effort and yields a significantly less positive return for a father when the teenager starts to contest limits, resist demands, and pull away for social independence. Now the man must rise to a difficult challenge: Stay closely connected to the son or daughter when he or she begins struggling to separate for freedom's sake.

As this process of change begins, usually between ages 9 and 13, a father typically encounters three problems that, depending on their resolution, can make parenting feel less rewarding than it was before. Each problem has the potential of discouraging the man from staying engaged with his adolescent son or daughter. There is the problem of *grief from loss,* the problem of *performance failure,* and the problem of *increased conflict.*

Of course, come the onset of the children's adolescence, a mother and father both face the same set of parental adjustments. However, because mothers tend to be the more committed parents, and because they have been more socialized to understand and manage close relationships, these problems tend to be less challenging issues for women than for men. In consequence, a mother is less likely than a father to pull away when the transformation of adolescence begins. The result is that if a father cannot toughen up and resolve each problem in a constructive (connecting) way, he is in danger of losing motivation to stay as involved with the adolescent as he was with the child. He is at risk of becoming more inattentive and inactive as a father during the teenage years.

THE PROBLEM OF GRIEF FROM LOSS

*"You used to be such a great kid,
what happened to you?"*

Consider a father whose little girl prizes special time with him, strives for his approval, believes he knows all the answers and can do no wrong, shares his interests to keep them close, laughs at his jokes, eagerly learns from his instruction, looks up to him, and does what he asks when he asks it. He is as entranced by his little daughter as she is adoring of him. "Parenting doesn't get any better than this," he tells his wife, and she agrees, knowing he's right. And she knows something else: this blissful companionship is not destined to last, because the ideal conditions of early fatherhood sooner or later will be moderated by the harder realities of adolescence.

For both this father and this little girl, adolescence begins with loss. As she starts to separate from childhood, to outgrow her previous definition of "little girl," to journey to young womanhood, to establish a world of friends socially independent from family, her father (love him as she still does) becomes more peripheral in her life. Now she prefers time with friends, acts like she cares less what he thinks, is more critical of his judgment, discounts his opinion when they disagree (which they do more often), is less interested in his interests, finds his humor embarrassing, resists his instruction, no longer idolizes him, and delays compliance in response to his requests.

For the father, looking back reveals an enormous loss: He will never have his daughter as little child again, never again share that special companionship, never again shine quite so brightly in her eyes. That golden period is past. The painful truth is that the father will miss old times they had together, the glad company they kept and the precious history they shared. Gone is his "little buddy" and "constant companion," suddenly (it seems to him) replaced by a more adversarial and distant adolescent who doesn't act like she misses him the way he misses her.

This apparent difference may even seem to him unfair. Doesn't she regret giving up the old way they used to be together? Yes, but she is growing on with her life, more inclined to looking forward to the future than to looking back at the past. The older, grown-up world that opens up before her is filled with new and exciting interests, experiences, and possibilities. While she eagerly anticipates the new, he feels bereft of the old. It's hard for him to appreciate progression in his daughter's growth when the cost of this progress is a very painful letting go.

What can make this transition even harder for the man is seeing his wife undergo the same loss, but with less troubling effect. While he feels disconnected from his daughter by her adolescent change, his wife (more deeply connected and committed as a mother) seems to be more accepting of this necessary loss, more able to process the pain, make parental adjustments, and move on.

At this inevitable separation point, what matters most for the future of his fathering involvement is how he deals with the grief such loss can bring. Honestly acknowledged, openly felt, and fully appreciated, this pain can be accepted as a normal part of growth: For child and parents, growing up requires giving up and letting go.

The resolution of this loss of child and childhood is to turn grief at what has been taken away into gratitude for what was given, and store the gifts of happy times in memory so that what was lost can be fondly recollected. Looking at old photographs of earlier times with his daughter, retelling each other funny stories about their adventures together, even an occasional visit to old haunts can all affirm for them both what was given that can never be taken away. "We sure had fun!" the daughter says. "We sure did!" her father agrees. If the father can claim some of the gifts that loss reveals, he becomes free to move on into a more challenging relationship with his daughter, becoming involved in new and different ways as she enters a more challenging period of growth.

What can cause the transition into adolescence to become disconnecting for a father is when his grief from loss is turned into anger at the adolescent for having changed. This is what can happen when he takes the adolescent alteration in his child personally, as an action taken meant to get or to get back at him. "She doesn't love me anymore!" "She's just doing this to get me upset!" Now he confuses direction with rejection and is in danger of rejecting back. This change in his daughter is *not* about rejection of the bond with her father; this change is about setting a new direction toward more independence.

Some men, because of the gender training they received, do not confront and process pain directly, and that includes not just physical pain but also experiential pain from loss. Acting uncaring to tough it out, they disguise from themselves and others hurt they feel. For example, a father having lost his beloved child to adolescence may guard against directly acknowledging and expressing grief by resorting to avoidance, apathy, or anger.

- In *avoidance,* he may say: "Well, if you don't have time for me anymore because of friends, then I'm too busy to have time for you."
- In *apathy,* he may say: "Well, if you don't care about doing old activities together anymore, then neither do I."
- In *anger,* he may say: "You used to be such a great kid, what's happened to you?"

Each statement from the father protects the man against feelings of loss and justifies disconnecting father from daughter as the adolescent passage begins. But it is better for him to openly acknowledge and accept what is a normal loss that comes with children growing up, and exercise the adult maturity required for moving on.

Three mature acts a father can take when he feels negatively stuck on his child's entry into adolescence are depersonalizing the change, seeing beneath the anger, and taking a positive initiative.

- To depersonalize the change, understand (as has been mentioned earlier) that because adolescence is such a self-centering process of growth, your son or daughter is too self-preoccupied and thoughtless of others to think about "getting" anyone, much less you. From here on through the rest of adolescence, she will be mostly concerned with getting *for* her self. Don't blame your daughter for the process of separation now underway.

- To defuse your anger, remember that men often use anger as a cover emotion to feel strong and to conceal from themselves and others more vulnerable states like disappointment, sadness, failure, hurt, helplessness, grief, and fear, for example. So ask yourself: "In addition to anger, what else am I feeling?" Then take the time to write or talk those emotions out. It's likely that your wife will listen and understand.

- To take a positive initiative, remember that the other side of loss is freedom—freedom *from* old limitations and freedom *for* new possibilities. Exploit the opportunities adolescent change create by suggesting new ways to be with your daughter, particularly around older interests she develops that neither of you could enjoy before.

THE PROBLEM OF PERFORMANCE FAILURE

*"What's the point of keeping after
a kid who refuses to do what I ask?"*

Consider a military officer, used to managing a company of soldiers that never questions orders, describing what it's like getting his 12-year-old son to accomplish simple chores around the home. "I'm so tired of delay and debate whenever I ask him to do anything, and then finally having him do it, but always partly or sloppily accomplished. How do you think this makes me feel? Able to command grown men into battle but unable to get my son to pick up his socks!"

A man's identity and self-worth are often tied up with the work he does, the position he occupies, the recognition he is given. Performance becomes a matter of personal pride. So the military father, in this example, is a successfully commanding man at work. Used to being in charge on the job, however, he faces daily insubordination at home, each act of teenage opposition a challenge to his authority and an insult to his pride. These experiences of frustration and failure in the family cause him to feel ineffective, incompetent, and unsuccessful as a father and a man. Some pride in performance in his fathering role has been lost, and with it a measure of self-respect.

Now a father may elect to disengage from parenting to reduce the painful sense of failure that he frequently feels from not performing with authority at home. This is where some "parental handoffs" occur, as he declares to his spouse that if his son's chores remain undone it's up to her to fix the problem. Yet by withdrawing from the field of supervision he has not only decreased standing and influence with his son, he has increased the parental burden on his wife.

The man feels like he has been demoted from being a successful father of an obedient child to a failed father of an unruly adolescent. Of course, now prone to finding faults in the parent who tends to be more critical of him, the adolescent can contribute to the man's diminished self-esteem with complaints about his father's performance: "You just push me to do well to make yourself look good!" And this accusation can strike home when the boy has a relationship-based mother who is sensitive to how he feels, and a performance-based father who seems to care most about how the boy achieves.

The resolution of feeling performance failure is for the father to recognize adolescence for what it is: an oppositional process that causes the young person to resist demands and push against restraints imposed by resident authorities in order to gain independence and create more freedom of choice. The fact that there is now more opposition and that the father finds himself prevailing in some encounters and yielding in others, is *not* a reflection of inferior performance. It is a statement about what happens when children rebel out of childhood and the *age of command* ("My parents have the power to determine what I choose to do") into adolescence and the *age of consent* ("My parents can't control me or stop me without my permission"). This is a powerful awakening that comes with adolescence, one that is as unwelcome to parents as it is liberating for the adolescent. There is a warning that is given by Steinberg & Levine early in their book *You & Your Adolescent* (1990) that fathers with a strong interest in retaining power of command during adolescence would do well to heed. "The parent-adolescent relationship is like a partnership in which the senior partner (the parent) has more expertise in many areas but looks forward to the day when the junior partner (the adolescent) will take over the business of running his or her own life. Parents who see the adolescent partnership as a losing proposition, or resist the adolescent's desire for self-determination, are asking for trouble."

"We can't control our child!" lament the parents as though this is a problem to be solved instead of a reality to accept. Of course, they never could control their child, not even in infancy. However, parenting is such a heavy responsibility, they wanted to believe in the illusion of control. So when they rocked the crying baby who then went peacefully to sleep, they thought: "We stopped the crying!" No they didn't. For reasons unknown, the baby decided to stop crying and parents took the credit for that decision. As for the child, he had his illusion of parental control too. "My parents make me do what they want by making rules!" He didn't realize how obedience was up to him. Come adolescence, that realization has arrived. "I used to think my parents controlled my freedom. Now I know better. My choices are really up to me."

Fathers who cannot understand and accept this transition into a more uncertain and embattled time with their teenager are at risk of wrongly attributing rising resistance to their own failure to perform as effective and controlling male authorities in the family. In counseling, it is common to have a father declare performance anxiety in response to parenting a teenager: "I can't make my son behave!" "That's okay," I reassure the man. "Parenting your children during adolescence is less about getting your way than about finding a way to influence the choices your teenager is determined to make."

THE PROBLEM OF INCREASED CONFLICT

*"Who wants to spend time with
a kid who only wants to argue?"*

Consider a father who, having grown up around bickering parents usually unable to resolve their differences, has a very low tolerance for conflict. He feels anxious when cross words are spoken. He wishes angry tensions would not arise. And he chooses to appease problems when he can, or avoid confrontation when he cannot. For this truly peace-loving man, his 15-year-old daughter, bristling with the combative energy that empowers so many mid-adolescents to fight for more social freedom, becomes a major source of unpleasant interaction. "I end up dreading the sound of the front door slamming when she gets home from school and I find myself tip-toeing around so I don't set her off. I just keep my distance and am happy when she's content to do the same." And so another father bows out of his adolescent's life when his salient male presence is actually just what she needs.

For fathers, the key to resolving the rising amount of conflict is to treat this increase not as a problem to be avoided, but as an opportunity to engage with your teenager in communication that can profit you both. Conflict is a time for you to take and explain stands that you want understood and to listen to what your teenager, in opposition, has to say about what she wants, perceives, values, or believes. If you are uncomfortable with conflict, your children's adolescence is a chance to get more used to it, to profit from the interchange, and to practice doing it safely and productively.

A father who approaches conflict as a discipline problem, by treating any disagreement from his teenagers as "talking back," loses two opportunities to connect with him. First, he loses a chance to communicate about a difference and create more mutual understanding, and second, he loses a chance to construct a mutually agreed upon resolution that strengthens the relationship.

Conflict with adolescents is *not* a discipline problem; but discipline (using instruction and correction to get consent) often involves conflict from confronting what did happen, what is happening, or what will happen. Family conflict is simply the process through which people confront and resolve inevitable human differences in relationships, communicating about them to better understand each other and sometimes making changes, concessions, or compromises to better get along.

There are two ways for family members to become intimately connected. The easy way is by sharing what they have in common, what they enjoy doing together, how they are alike. The harder way is by understanding and accommodating how they are different, and this way involves some level of conflict—from mild disagreements to major arguments. A father who treats conflict with his teenagers as a punishable offense shuts half of intimacy down. "My dad never really got to know me because he wouldn't let me disagree."

Conflict has both educational and training value. Conflict has educational value because it results from two different ways of looking at the same issue. Through discussion, conflict can open up an exchange of ideas that can educate you both about each other. Using conflict to explore a difference, you come to know each other more deeply than you did before. "We need to talk about how we see violence in video gaming very differently. The killing that just horrifies me is just having fun for you."

Conflict also has training value. How you repeatedly choose to engage in conflict has a rehearsal effect. By your example and instruction in many conflicts over time, your teenager not only learns how to conduct conflict with you, but he carries those habits of behavior into other relationships. For example, from experiencing disagreements with you, your teenager may learn to listen with an open mind and not tune out, interrupt, or walk away. This training is just one essential component in the curriculum of family life that shapes adolescent behavior for adult life. Every time you engage in conflict with your teenager, you are preparing this adult-in-training for conducting conflict in the future. Avoid conflict with your adolescent and not only do you lose an opportunity for learning about your teenager and training your teenager in the constructive management of disagreement, you may be passing on the habit of conflict avoidance.

Why is there more conflict during adolescence? As your son or daughter begins objecting to old restraints, developing new interests, and experimenting with new identities, you have to decide which differences in wants, behaviors, beliefs, and values you are willing to accept, and which you are determined to challenge. Oppose the ones you will not tolerate (these days body piercing is a common concern, but the rebellion can be anything new or different) and this specific encounter can quickly assume symbolic importance representing a very inflammatory issue: personal freedom. Explodes the teenager: "It's my body and I should be able to do what I want with it!"

In addition, the compliance and cooperation of yesteryear has become the active (argument) and passive (delay) resistance of today. A lot of the times, you have to be willing and ready to set and patrol responsible boundaries in which your teenager, older now but still a child, is still expected to live. So with your sustained insistence (relentless nagging) you wear the teenager's resistance down, until to get you off his back, he reluctantly completes his household chores.

In the example of the father who grew up with bickering parents, we end up with a man who hates conflict more than he loves his daughter, who backs off important stands, shies away from discussing significant differences, and is reluctant to keep after her about what needs to get done. The result is that she learns to override disagreement rather than listen and work it through. To pick up the slack, his wife may confront more of the differences with their daughter. The woman is frequently less easily put off or threatened by conflict because it is an ingrained part of her feminine, relational way. While she may be more comfortable listening and responding to the expression of strong feelings, the father may prefer explanation and reasonable discussion to keep intensity restrained. So in a heated confrontation with their teenager, the mother asks, "How are you feeling?" to hear emotion out, while the father asks, "Why are you feeling that way?" to bring emotion under rational control.

In my own experience counseling families, there is more conflict between mothers and teenagers than between fathers and teenagers, usually because the mother is more willing to take on the adolescent in conflict. Some of the research on gender differences in marital conflict tends to support this impression. "The question is raised whether males withdraw from marital conflict primarily because they have difficulty dealing with conflict.... The article concludes that the withdrawal behavior adopted by men during high levels of marital conflict does appear to enable them to maintain power in the relationship." (See Noller, in the *Journal of Language and Social Psychology,* vol. 12, no. 1–2, 1993.) The article identifies male withdrawal behavior and links it to the maintenance of power; when engagement gets too hard to bear, the father keeps himself apart from and above the family fray.

Loss of the beloved child to the more abrasive adolescent, anxiety that one's performance as a parent is less effective, and more conflict during adolescence all can discourage fathers from maintaining full parental involvement during the difficult teenage years. It requires commitment, maturity, and courage to stay connected during the adolescent passage, with little appreciation from your teenager for the time and effort it takes. Later, however, when your son or daughter has some perspective, it is not uncommon for the grown child to say: "Dad, Mom, thanks for hanging in there with me during those hard times."

CONNECTING IS A TWO-WAY STREET

Having identified some common reasons a father might disconnect, it is important to note that your teenager has some responsibility for connecting, too. You can do a lot to build a strong relationship, but you can't do it all. So here is what a father might say to his teenager to enlist his help:

"During your passage out of childhood toward adulthood, there will be many changes in yourself and in me. As you push for more independence, I will struggle over decisions about when it is necessary to hold you back and when it is safe to let you go, and there will be more conflict between us. Your job is to manage your relationship with me to get the freedom you need to grow. Part of my job is to tell you how to accomplish this objective.

"First, you must understand change. Growth is change—the experience of moving from old to new, from the same to different, from familiar to unfamiliar, from known to unknown. Adolescence is change. To yourself and to me, you are no longer the old, same, familiar, known child that you used to be. Now you are becoming a new, different, unfamiliar, and unknown person for me to live with. This transformation is very important for you to understand, because as you change in your teen years, I change my parenting in response.

"To your becoming *new* in some ways, I miss some of the 'old' child I knew. Feeling sad and lonely from this loss, I may hold on to the way you used to be to resist the change.

"To your becoming *different,* I have to make some adjustments I don't like. Feeling angry, I may act critical of your change. To your becoming *unfamiliar,* I'll find you hard to get used to. Feeling awkward, I may act uncomfortable with your change. To your becoming *unknown,* I'll find my ignorance hard to tolerate. Feeling fearful, I may act worried by your change.

"You need to be sensitive to the impact of your adolescence on me if you want to help create a relationship that provides you with the increased independence you desire. So to keep me supportive of your growth, try doing the following and see if it doesn't serve you well.

"To reduce my feelings of sadness over losing.you as a child, give me expressions of caring.

"To reduce my feelings of anger about adjustments I have to make, give me more cooperation and helpfulness. To reduce my feelings of awkwardness about how to relate, give me new ways to be with you. To reduce my feelings of fear from ignorance, give me adequate and accurate information about what's going on.

"When you bring it down to basics, managing me during your adolescence is not that difficult to do. Understand your challenge: to keep me feeling connected to you while adolescence is pushing and pulling us apart.

"Remember: When I feel disconnected from you, I can be really hard to live with. The more disconnected I feel, the more ignorant (worried) and negative (critical) and controlling (restrictive) I tend to become. And who enjoys living with a dad like that? So don't deliberately disconnect from me unless you want this unhappy outcome to occur.

"Instead, to keep me feeling connected, just remember to do four things:

1.   Give me expressions of caring;
2.   Give me acts of cooperation;
3.   Give me opportunities for contact;
4.   Give me continuing communication.

The more connected you help me feel during your adolescence, the easier it becomes for you to get the support, freedom, and independence from me that you need to grow. You do this for me and I will try to be reasonable to work with."

CHAPTER THREE

THE PROBLEM WITH WORK

Children learn to judge your degree of caring and commitment as a father not so much by what you say as by how you act. They know the difference between a promise maker and a promise keeper, between a dad who doesn't do what he says and a dad who is as good as his word.

To stay connected to your teenagers, *be there* by being a dad they can count on. Meet your commitments to them. Make the effort and take the time to be present at their events. Support them with your help. Be available to talk about what matters to them. Listen to what they have to say. It's hard to feel connected to a dad who *isn't there,* who is unreliable, uninterested, uninvolved, and uncommunicative.

One common cause for disconnection can be a father's overriding attachment to work. As mentioned earlier, a father can certainly demonstrate his love by faithfully working to help support his family. However, fathers have to watch out that work does not become so all-consuming and all-important that it disconnects the man from those he loves.

Gender trained to define himself more around performance than relationships, a man's commitment to work, to job, to position, and to career is really just an expression of dedication to himself. This last statement does *not* include the dad who is working multiple jobs to piece together a living to support a family.

I am talking about the father for whom identification and involvement with a job become the defining preoccupations in his life, for whom the world of work commands more personal investment and yields more personal satisfaction than his role in the family.

It can be hard for men to keep the importance and payoffs of work performance in perspective. Because of their different attachment histories with their children and different sex-role socialization growing up, men tend to be more prone to sacrifice family for job and career than mothers, who are more prone to do the reverse. In the *2005 American Time Use Survey* (see Bureau of Labor Statistics, July 17, 2006), data show that men put in longer hours on the job than women, and that women put in significantly more family time on household and childcare work than men.

When occupation, career, or position is a primary attachment for a father, there is always the risk that it can become an excuse to evade responsible involvement with family and parenting, particularly during the more distant, resistant, and challenging adolescent years. Consider three common ways that fathers evade responsibility and disconnect from their teenagers:

- They spend time on the job at the expense of time with family, the excuse of: *"I'm too busy."*
- They allow the duress of the job to create stress in the family, the excuse of: *"I've hard a hard day."*
- They give their best self at work but not at home, the excuse of: *"I can act any way I feel with family."*

SPENDING TIME ON THE JOB AT THE EXPENSE OF TIME WITH FAMILY

"I'm too busy."

The following fable (see Pickhardt 2004) illustrates how a father's career can become a powerful excuse for absenting himself from daily involvement with children.

The Man Who Worked So Hard For His Family

The man who worked so hard for his family that he barely saw them was missed by those who wished he'd be around some more, and not act so grouchy when he finally got home, only wanting to be left alone to enjoy his drinks and watch TV and have a little peace and quiet for God's sakes. Didn't they understand a man was tired after working twelve-hour days and weekends at the office, killing himself to be successful to keep them happy? How could they complain that he wasn't doing enough with them when for birthdays and Christmas they got more than anybody else they knew? He saw to that. What did they want, blood?

No. It was his company that they wanted, but his questions caused the family to feel guilty for wanting to see him more. They tried to feel grateful for the small amount of time they did see him. Except the very youngest child, who still felt disappointed when he broke special promises because he had to work late again, and felt rejected when he seemed to prefer time with the job to time with her, and felt angry that she wasn't supposed to feel angry at him for working so much since it was never his fault. The importance of his career made him do it!

One thing was sure, she told him. She never wanted to work like he did if this was what it did to people. He was appalled: Was she actually suggesting that he chose to work so hard because that was what he wanted?

Oh no, she apologized. Of course nobody who really loved their family would ever work so hard at not seeing them!

It's hard for family to argue against the sanctity of a father's work. It's hard to criticize the time away from home your employment takes when what you earn supports or helps support the family. It's hard to fault a father for working hard at his job. Like the daughter in the fable, it's easy for children to feel guilty that they want to see you more. However, if you want to stay connected to your teenagers, you must provide evidence of involvement to show that your fathering of them matters at least as much or more than your work.

The man in the fable is a good provider of financial support, but he evades personal responsibility in three ways. He blames the job for his lack of fathering, claiming that it takes all his time and energy. He blames the job for his physical absence from the family, thereby disowning any measure of personal choice over the long hours he puts in. He also makes it sound as though he works for his family when he mostly works to satisfy and glorify himself. It would be much cleaner for all concerned for this dad to honestly declare: "My career is my most important interest. I want to put it first, and then do what I can to be a father when I am home."

Typically, a father has two provider responsibilities. Working a job to help support family is certainly one, but remaining actively involved as husband and father is another. Finding the balance between commitment to job and commitment to home is never easy. To a degree, his job does make requirements he cannot refuse, as he should explain to his teenagers so they understand why he cannot always be present in their lives as much as he or they would like. "When I sell my services to an employer in exchange for salary I'm paid, I give up some personal freedom. Now the organization has bought my time and effort, and I have to work on terms they set. So although I wish I could be at all your games, some days I do have to work late and so cannot attend."

You must find a balance between the minimum commitment required to hold your job and the maximum effort needed to get ahead. You must continually review the boundary you have created because work can be seductive. The force of never-ending job demands, and the temptation to give non-required time and extra effort to get more done, can subtly upend the healthy balance between family and work. You start to leave for the office a little earlier, you stay a little later, and you bring a little more work home; as you do, distance grows between you and your family. It is up to you to set sufficient boundaries on work so you have active time and energy for your teenagers.

What can help keep susceptibility to overwork in check is awareness of the difference between what you *choose* to do and what you *have* to do. Thinking you "have to" suggests you are a victim of your employment, but understanding that you "choose to" owns some measure of discretionary choice. It is by taking responsibility for discretionary choice on the job that you can moderate time there so you have adequate time at home.

When it comes to fathering, there really is no substitute for showing up. If you have a job that involves a lot of travel, there are things you can do to show you're still available. If you are physically separated from your teenagers, give them a wake-up call in the morning and wish them a great day. E-mail them something about where you are. At night call again to see how their days went, and even have them fax homework to you so you can give them long-distance help.

ALLOWING DURESS OF THE JOB TO CREATE STRESS IN THE FAMILY

"I've had a hard day."

Think about the variety of pressures your job can create. For openers: too much demand, too little support, inadequate information, revised responsibilities, unfair treatment, undeserved blame, lack of credit, poor evaluations, continual interruptions, sudden deadlines, unrealistic expectations, broken commitments, constant reorganization, employment insecurity, internal competition, changing plans, unproductive meetings, insensitive superiors, unreliable peers, incompetent subordinates, rude customers, unreasonable clients, rising quotas, unreachable numbers, anxious moments, endless frustrations, little insults, hurtful conflicts, suppressed injuries, and stored-up angers. When you sell your services to an organization the demands of the system take precedence over the needs and preferences of the individual because employees are paid to subordinate what they would like to do to what they are told to do.

Jobs are stressful. So what else is new? Maybe this: Stress is contagious. In her article "Secondhand Stress," Caroline Hwang (*Ladies' Home Journal,* July 2006) writes: "To be sure, dealing with someone else's stress is, well, stressful. . . . In effect, another person's stress can spread like secondhand smoke: It can become your problem because you're there."

Unless you are careful, you can come home from a hard day at work loaded up with stress, and unload it on family members to feel better. Now they are feeling stressed as well, and you find yourself disconnected from those you love because the father your teenagers were looking forward to seeing has become a person no one wants to be around. To protect their well-being, they distance themselves from you.

Over the years, I have developed a model for explaining stress and the contagion of stress. As the demands at work wind you up, wear you down, and sap your energy, there are four common levels of stress to watch out for.

Level one: *fatigue*. Fatigue from being overspent ultimately creates a *negative outlook* on the world. Discouraged and depleted from his day at work, a man is more likely to notice what is going wrong rather than what is positive in his life, expecting the worst to happen and not the best. For example: A 12-year-old boy rushes up to show his fatigued father, who cares a lot about performance, a report card that is all A's and B's and one C. "Where did this C come from?" demands the man, ignoring the better grades. "You're not going to be allowed to go anywhere until you bring this up!" Wanting praise and getting a reprimand, the son sadly turns and walks away, disconnecting from the dad who could have used the restorative hug the boy was prepared to give.

Level two has to do with *pain* from daily frustration. Accumulated incidents of stress have the capacity to wound, creating over-sensitivity. Anxious moments and aggravations during his day can turn into nagging tensions and aches that cause increased vulnerability to further slights and small adversities that arise. Already feeling hurt, he is more easily upset. For example: Entering the home, instead of finding soothing peace and quiet, the pain-ridden father is greeted by an assault of music blaring through his 16-year-old daughter's open bedroom door, sound that rubs him raw. "Turn that noise off!" be barks. And his daughter, who was feeling happy to have him home and would have acted welcoming, just coldly shuts the door behind him as he leaves.

The third level of stress involves *burnout*. Having given so much of himself to endless demands at work, the man lacks of motivation to give any more, creating an *insensitivity* to things that would normally matter. He seems not to care. For example: The man's wife relates some concerns to him about the kids, but because he is so bereft of further energy to be attentive, after five minutes of whatever she was describing, he asks: "What were you saying?" This is when his wife explodes: "What was I saying? You mean you haven't heard a word I've said?" She feels hurt by his insensitivity. He didn't even care enough to listen. Now his wife disconnects from him, just like the kids.

The final level of stress is *breakdown* from incapacity to function as one normally could. Physically this can mean becoming easily sick and having a hard time recovering. Emotionally it can mean becoming caught in the toils of chronic worry, severe anxiety, despondency, or depression. Socially it can mean isolating oneself. In any case, it causes an inability to function as a contributing family member. Here's an example: Left alone by family members his stress has pushed away, he seeks chemical and electronic relief in social isolation. He pours himself a stiff drink, goes into the bedroom, shuts the door, and turns on the TV, becoming unavailable for family interaction. At home, he's really not at home at all. He's far away, part of that distance created by family members who have decided they're better off letting him keep his own company. Now he is completely disconnected from those whose expressions of love, were they available, could help him recover from the hard day he has had.

To review how the man's experience with the four stages of stress became contagious to others:

- Fatigue caused him to become negative and act *critical* of his son.
- Pain caused him to become over-sensitive and act *irritable* with his daughter.
- Burnout caused him to become insensitive and act *unresponsive* to his wife.
- Breakdown caused him to isolate and become *unavailable* to his entire family.

To keep this unhappy scenario from unfolding for you after a taxing day at work, take transitional responsibility. Institute some non-chemical strategies for taking time for the three R's—relaxation, renewal, and recovery—before you re-enter the family, ready to positively engage with the challenging world of adolescents awaiting at home.

The transition doesn't have to take long. It can be a quiet commute listening to music. It can be a break to exercise, to read the paper, to socialize with coworkers before leaving, to do whatever it takes to unwind, let go, and look forward to coming home during a vulnerable family time of day when everyone else is tired and worn out, too. What won't work for you is ignoring stress and stressing family by bringing a hard day home.

GIVING ONE'S BEST AT WORK BUT NOT AT HOME

"I can act any way I feel with family."

Listen to this father describe the difference between conducting himself at work and conducting himself at home. "On the job, I have to be
careful how I treat people because who I upset can get me in trouble, so
I watch how I act. And of course with customers I have to be on best
behavior because I don't want to blow a sale. But at home it's different.
I'm free to let down, let go, and act any way I feel, no matter how, because they're my family and will put up with me no matter what."

Yes, they may tolerate his poor treatment, but they won't like him
for acting in uncaring and unloving ways. However, this man is pro-
ceeding on a very common false assumption that many fathers share.
Work relationships require effort because employees are paid to fulfill a
service, while at home less effort is required since love is unconditional
and family membership is secure. Carried to its worst extreme, this distinction can lead to a division between the public man who is beloved
for his good works and the private man who secretly abuses his family.
I can testify from counseling that this phenomenon is more common
than many people would like to believe.

Consider a more moderate example of this problem. A husband,
wife, and two teenage sons are seated around a supper table. The
mother and sons bow their heads, eating quietly, while their father,
who spends his days making high-dollar sales, rails at the sons' adolescent shortcomings and complains about the food, only getting angrier
should anyone dare to speak. Then the telephone rings. He picks it up
and is immediately transformed into a genial, humorous, considerate
man who anyone would be happy to meet. "No, no problem calling
me at home, no problem at all. Glad you did. Always happy to talk to a
new customer. How can I help you?" And for almost ten minutes the
sons observe their father doing what he does so well, greeting a new ac-
quaintance like an old friend. Finally he hangs up, but before the familiar glare returns to his eyes, one of his sons asks: *"Dad, how come you
treat strangers better than us?"*

Actions speak louder than words when it comes to demonstrating
priorities, which in this case clearly imply that someone who pays the

man money deserves better treatment than family members who love him. So if you're a father who believes that people in the workplace deserve your best effort, and what's left is good enough for your family even if it's bad, think again. With adolescents, what you model is what you get. Thus for the father in this supper table vignette, the harsh and dismissive conduct that he models is likely what he will encourage in return. If he wants his sons to make the effort to treat him well, that is the effort he must make with them. If he wishes to stay well connected to them, he needs to give his family his *best* behavior, never his worst.

"Courtesy" is a term that describes the code of caring conduct a father needs to follow at home. It's an old-fashioned word that may sound out of date, but the consideration you show demonstrates the effort that you make to treat other people well.

Courtesy behaviors are those small gestures that define how thoughtfully people treat each other on a daily basis. For example, would your teenagers rather be told to help or be asked to help? Would you rather be interrupted by your teenagers or be listened to when saying something important? Would your partner rather be ignored or be noticed for special efforts made? Would your teenagers rather be criticized or be complimented when performing their best? Would you rather be taken for granted or be thanked for doing them a favor? Would you rather be untouched or hugged when feeling disappointed from work? Asking, listening, noticing, complimenting, thanking, and hugging are just a few acts of common courtesy that all contribute to quality of family life by causing the giver to act thoughtfully and the receiver to feel like they're being treated with consideration.

Let's focus on these questions in another way. What can happen to your teenagers when no one is courteous? How would they end up feeling if you continually told them what to do, interrupted when they were trying to speak, ignored their special efforts, criticized their performance, took it for granted when they did you a favor, and didn't hug them when they were feeling sad?

Through lack of basic courtesy, other people's feelings can get hurt. Why? Because small acts of inconsiderate behavior represent important symbolic qualities. For example, your lack of listening can signify a lack of acceptance for your teenager: "Dad is never open to hearing what I have to say!" Your lack of simple thanks can signify a lack of appreciation to your teenager: "Dad doesn't value anything I do!" Your lack of touch can signify a lack of affection to your teenager: "Dad doesn't love me, I can tell!" Your lack of compliments can signify a lack of approval to your teenager: "Nothing I do ever pleases Dad!" Little courtesy behaviors are big things in disguise because they signify larger meanings. This is why courtesy means a lot. It is also why your colleagues and clients at work are not the only ones who deserve it. Remember your family at home.

Courtesy counts because it conveys larger caring in a host of little ways, because omissions can hurt, and because these specific acts are laden with symbolic value. President Kennedy's notion of "grace under pressure" is a worthwhile fathering goal to consider. At the worst of times strive to act your best, asserting family leadership by keeping courtesy up under family duress or when life at work has you down. If you treat your teenagers as *guests in your relationship,* observing the little courtesies that signify so much, your connection should be strong enough to weather the normal strains of adolescent growth.

Remember, when it comes to your job or career:

- Don't use work as an excuse to absent yourself from family;
- Don't bring stress from work home to stress your family;
- Don't treat those at home with any less consideration than you give your boss or your best customer at work.

CHAPTER FOUR

CLARIFYING EXPECTATIONS FOR ADOLESCENT CHANGE

Usually beginning during the ages of 9 to 13 (this means in late elementary school), your child's entry into adolescence and the race to independence begins. And a race it is, because teenagers tend to be in a hurry to grow up. As a father you're not even sure of the general course this race will follow, much less the obstacles along the way. All you know is that your child has started to become different and more difficult to live with. This is no time for you to be too busy with work (see chapter 3) to attend to the unfolding changes in your son or daughter. If there are two parents in the home, you need *both* hands on deck to share the perplexity as you wonder just what is happening and what you should be doing in response. What is causing your child's more intense, erratic, and abrasive behavior? *What has adolescence done to your child?*

THE PROBLEM OF DENIAL

Most parents in general, and fathers in particular, are woefully unprepared for their child's adolescence, which, in their denial, they believe won't happen, or is only going to happen to other people's children. No. All children have to grow through it, and all parents have to get used to it. To help overcome your denial, try answering the following questions about your experiences growing up. Do you remember:

1. Wanting your parents to stop treating you as a child?
2. Thinking your parents didn't understand you?
3. Arguing more with your parents and resenting their authority?
4. Wishing your body would start looking more grown-up?
5. Becoming more preoccupied with personal appearance and dress?
6. Not liking the way you looked?
7. Feeling unpopular for not having friends or the friends you wanted?
8. Testing, getting around, and beating "the system?"
9. Putting off parental requests and breaking parental rules?
10. Wanting to stay up later at night and sleep in later in the day?
11. Not working hard at school or just hard enough to get by?
12. Not telling your parents everything that was going on?
13. Sneaking out after your parents were asleep?
14. Getting into more fights with your parents?
15. Sometimes lying to parents to do the forbidden or to get out of trouble?
16. Shoplifting or stealing to see what you could get away with?
17. Daring something risky, getting away with it, or getting hurt?
18. Wanting to spend more time with friends than with family?
19. Experimenting with tobacco, alcohol, or other substances?
20. Being more interested in sex?
21. Hating being bored and loving excitement?
22. Going along with the group when that really wasn't what you wanted to do?
23. Making impulsive decisions in the moment that you had later cause to regret?
24. Wanting to engage in adult activities?
25. Doing something illegal to get the freedom you desired?

If you answered "Yes" to many of these questions, all I can tell you is that adolescence hasn't changed, and that many of the ways you felt, believed, and behaved back then, your teenagers will be feeling and thinking and acting now.

Denial is the enemy-in-hiding. Denial is refusing to acknowledge what really happened, is happening, or is going to happen. The purpose of denial is to protect a person from admitting and dealing with an unwanted, disturbing, or painful truth or event. The problem with denial is that it disables people from engaging with what did go on or is going on, and it enables problematic behavior by covering it up or allowing it to continue. Early parental denial of teenage substance abuse is a good example. Not wanting to believe their son's self-defeating behavior is chemically influenced (he's quit sports and started skipping school), they look for any other explanation, testing him for a learning disability, ADHD, even depression. They refuse to believe that someone in their family would do drugs.

Accept it: Adolescence is a rite of passage. "The forms of adolescent rites of passage vary greatly; however, the need for separation, involvement of an elder, transition, and a recognized change in status is clear. These elements are found ubiquitously in human beings at this stage of life. If our society does not adequately provide for these needs in a formalized structure, young people will seek to create their own rites. These attempts may be partially successful, but often are disastrous." (See Delaney in *Adolescence,* winter, 1995.) *Fathers, stay connected to your adolescents so you can help direct a safe and healthy passage to adulthood.*

The first key to fathering a teenager is to get informed about adolescence so you can be prepared for normal challenges, changes, and conflicts when they come.

The 10- to 12-year process of adolescence begins in late elementary school and doesn't end until the young person's early to mid-twenties. You may well ask: "Does this mean I've got another 12 years of adolescence to go with our rebellious 10-year-old?" Indeed. In our highly diverse, individualistic, complex, changeable society, adolescence is not some overnight alteration that suddenly confers on a child the readiness to assume adult status and shoulder adult responsibilities. It may well be in simpler, smaller, more homogenous, more traditional, more stable societies, that children can accomplish this adult transformation through a short ceremonial rite of passage, and emerge prepared to inhabit and carry forward the same social and occupational roles as their parents. "In primitive cultures, early responsibility and status are given to youths, whose puberty is appropriately and ceremoniously marked. Interestingly, adolescence in such cultures is usually a mild period. In our society, with its complexity, demands and codes, we postpone recognition of adolescents as adults, hinder their independence, frustrate a biologically sexually mature organism." (See Teicher, "Normal Psychological Changes in Adolescence," in *California Medicine*, vol. 85, no. 3, 1956.)

The United States, however, and many other highly industrialized countries today, are not small, simple, or static. I believe we pay a price for our freedom of individual choice, richness of social complexity, cultural diversity, and accelerating social change, and an extended adolescence for our children is one way we pick up this cost. So, while encouraging responsibility in your teenager, be patient with all the travails it takes before full independence can be claimed. The long time required for growing up today is not a problem to complain about, but a reality to work with and accept, including acceptance that your active parenting responsibility will probably last longer than your parents' responsibility did for you. And if you have a child in your forties, you will be acting as father to an adolescent in your sixties.

Although your teenager's unruly passages toward independence will seem confusing to you much of the time, let me give you a sense of the process by describing common growth changes and statements that I typically see and hear in counseling, roughly unfolding year by adolescent year.

- A nine-year-old who used to be full of creative energy seems to have entered "developmental lumphood," and just lays around, frustrated and complaining that there's nothing to do, but resents it when you offer work at home that would be of help. *"I'm too tired, leave me alone!"*
- A ten-year-old who was always efficient about getting homework done now fails to bring assignments home or, having done so, fails to turn them in. *"I just forgot!"*

- An 11-year-old has decided to give up a beloved sport because it's suddenly become childish to play. *"I'm too old to do that kid stuff anymore!"*
- A 12-year-old blames getting in trouble on being treated unfairly. *"It's not my fault, it's your stupid rule!"*
- A 13-year-old who appears unable to converse with parents for five minutes can communicate for hours to friends on the phone or over the computer. *"There's nothing much to say to parents, but with friends I can talk forever!"*
- A 14-year-old whose room the health department would condemn defends living in such an anarchic mess as a right of self-determination: *"If you don't like how I keep my room, keep out!"*
- A 15-year-old protests honesty after not having told parents the whole story. *"It's not lying if I only answer what you think to ask!"*
- A 16-year-old uses so many ways of evading direct communication that parents can never find a good time to talk—a bad time being the best time they can get: *"Not now, can't you see I'm busy!"*
- A 17-year-old with a part-time job after school resents curfew limits more than ever. *"If I can make my own money, I should be able to run my own life!"*
- An 18-year-old senior with a desire to go to college keeps putting off completing applications until the deadline is almost passed. *"I'll start on them next weekend!"*
- A 19-year-old, who is now working and living in an apartment, is furious to discover his or her old bedroom has now been converted for other family use: *"I can't believe you took away my room!"*
- A 20-year-old feels harassed by bill collectors calling about unpaid credit card balances. *"Why don't they leave me alone!"*
- A 21-year-old college junior loses another job from oversleeping and arriving late to work. *"I can't help being late when I'm hungover from the night before!"*
- A 22-year-old keeps falling into unhappy love. *"No matter how good they start out, all my relationships end up badly!"*
- A 23-year-old wants to come back and live at home for a while after losing a job or flunking out of college, incurring credit debt or defaulting on a lease. *"I need to start over!"*

KNOWING WHAT TO EXPECT IS IMPORTANT

These predicaments and endless others like them cause many fathers to long for the good old days of childhood when they could trust a son or daughter to act as anticipated and desired. But an adolescent is *not* a child. An adolescent is an instinctively and intentionally different person, and unless you can adjust your expectations accordingly and accept this new reality, you are setting yourself up for unnecessary stress, putting yourself at risk of emotionally overreacting and making a hard situation worse.

It is important to factor into your fathering an appreciation of the power of expectations, understanding what they are and how they function. What I am going to describe is a model I developed for parents to help them appreciate how their expectations about adolescent change can have powerful emotional consequences on the parenting they do, for good or ill.

The model is this. Your expectations are *mental sets* that help you anticipate change. Consider three kinds of mental sets:

- Predictions: What you think *will* happen
- Ambitions: What you *want* to have happen
- Conditions: What you believe *should* happen

These mental sets are chosen, not genetically determined, and they are functional. They help you move through time (from now to later) and through change (from old to new) so that the reality you encounter is to some degree the reality you expected. Expectations are essential for preparation: "I thought this might happen." With no capacity to form expectations, blanket ignorance about what is going to happen can generate panic: "I never know what's going to happen next!"

For many fathers, expectations that fit how your son or daughter once believed and behaved as a child may not fit the reality of how he or she typically changes during adolescence.

- A prediction—"My child *will* always tell me the truth";
- An ambition—"I *want* my child to communicate a lot to me so we can feel close";

- A condition—"My child *should* comply with adult rules."

To the degree the child fit these expectations, you:

- felt *secure* your prediction was met ("I get good information");
- felt *satisfied* your ambition was fulfilled ("My child talks to me a lot");
- felt *in charge* when your conditions were obeyed ("My child does what he/she is told").

Come adolescence, however, these old expectations may not fit the new reality of how your son or daughter sometimes acts. Now she may lie more often for freedom's sake (see Walbridge, "On Lying in Adolescence," *ParentingAdolescents.com,* 2006.) Now she may communicate with you less for more privacy's sake. "One way adolescents establish their emotional independence is by keeping their thoughts and feelings to themselves." (See Steinberg & Levine, *You & Your Adolescent,* 1990.) Now she may break more rules for rebellion's sake. "The youth rebels against his conscience, flaunts new freedom, verbalizes his contempt for its demands, and acts out token proof that he is free of it. In seeking a symbol of his conscience against which to strike, he most frequently chooses his parents." (See Teicher in *California Medicine,* vol. 85, no. 3, 1956.)

Unless you build these changes into your expectations,

- you are likely to feel *anxious* from surprise when your prediction of honesty is violated;
- you are likely to feel *sad* from disappointment when your ambition of close communication is violated;
- and you are likely to feel *angry* from betrayal when your condition of obedience is violated.

Mental sets, like expectations, have emotional consequences, particularly when they don't fit the reality you anticipated. You must either change your expectations to fit the new reality of adolescence, or risk overreacting in response. Overreactions occur when you not only have to confront your adolescent's dishonesty, distance, and disobedience (as a responsible father should), but you also have to deal with the emotional costs of your violated expectations as well—the anxiety, sadness, and anger that you feel.

Remember that *expect* does not mean *accept.* "Expect" means being prepared by anticipating common adolescent changes so that, should they occur, you are not taken by total surprise and can deal with them in a calm and effective manner. If you know what to expect, then you won't waste emotional energy when misconduct occurs. You will reduce the likelihood that you will overreact. "I don't like how my son lied to me to get out of chores, but I'm not surprised, given his age. And I'm prepared to help him get back on a truthful path."

One way to begin building realistic expectations to anticipate the process of adolescence is to break it down into three large sequential phases:

- The separation from childhood;
- The redefinition of identity;
- The departure into independence.

In each phase, a new set of developmental differences is expressed, each of which creates emotional vulnerabilities for your teenager to manage. As a father, these are vulnerabilities you must be sensitive to.

PHASE ONE: THE SEPARATION FROM CHILDHOOD

With the expression of more oppositional differences, the boy or girl signifies that the separation from childhood has begun. Rebelling out of childhood is how adolescence begins, and in words and actions these separation statements express the motivation to change.

- "I am *different* from how I was as a child."
- "I want to be treated *differently* from when I was a child."
- "I am going to treat you *differently* than I did as a child."
- "I am *different* from how you are as my parents."
- "I am going to act *differently* from how you want me to behave."
- "I am going to become *different* from how you want me to be."

There are two problems associated with these statements. Because they are oppositional, the adolescent now has more trouble fitting into the family, and finds him- or herself at risk of getting into more disagreements with you and receiving more of your disapproval ("How many times do I have to ask you to get something done before you finally do it?"). In addition, when you express intolerance of some of these differences, and oppose the child's behavior to show you have had all the change you will accept ("You're not leaving this house dressed that way!"), the adolescent can feel alienated from you. The teenager may use this alienation as a badge of adolescent status, but also pays an emotional price. More criticized by parents, the adolescent can feel like a misfit, rejected and isolated at home. Now acceptance in family can feel more insecure.

The separation from childhood creates the emotional vulnerability of loneliness at home. At this point, the boy or girl is at higher risk of depending on friends (who are all feeling "different" in the same way) for acceptance to compensate for loss of affiliation with family. To respect this vulnerability, keep communicating interest in the adolescent as a person and providing affirmation at a time when you typically must take more frequent issue with his or her oppositional behavior.

Remember to be nonjudgmental in your correction, focusing not on disapproval, but disagreement: *"I disagree with choices you have made, this is why, and this is what needs to happen in consequence."* Correction is criticism enough. Negative evaluation just injures fragile self-esteem.

In response to brazen statements of independence like "I don't care about being with family," a father needs to read beneath the surface of the empty boast; it usually means "I still want you to want time with me, but I know I'm too old to admit it!" In response to statements of disinterest in or objections to participating in family functions, a father can be tempted to not include the adolescent in family functions: "Why let her spoil the rest of us having fun?" Social exclusion is a mistake. Pursue participation in family events with repeated invitations to show that you want and value the teenager's company, and that the teenager is a valued and integral part of the family—still the primary social group to which he or she belongs. More often than not he or she will end up finally accepting your offer and having a good time in spite of earlier protests to the contrary. When you let the teenager reject normal membership at home, you raise his or her risk of switching primary social affiliation from family to friends, undercutting your own parental influence in the process.

> *What not to say:* "If you don't want to be with us, then I don't want to be with you."
> *What to say:* "Even though you don't feel like it, please join us and come along."

PHASE TWO: THE REDEFINITION OF IDENTITY

With the expression of trial differences, the boy or girl, through words and actions, announces that the redefinition of identity has begun. Obvious change becomes a regular occurrence. Appearance, dress, cultural heroes, social fads, music, relationships, interests, and aspirations can each be all-important one day only to be dismissed the next.

A father can get impatient with the fleeting nature of some interests and the enduring presence of others. In both cases, however, these are *trial,* not *terminal* differences that allow the adolescent to experiment with a host of different ways of appearing and behaving and believing, in the process sorting out just who he or she authentically is. To be so changeable and to be caught in-between being no longer quite a child but not yet quite an adult is to feel awkward, and to create the emotional vulnerability of self-consciousness.

During the redefinition of identity, acute self-consciousness can make the child more vulnerable to criticism. In addition, these are the years when teasing or put-downs, particularly in public, can inflict their deepest damage, leaving young people not only feeling humiliated but, even worse, incorporating the demeaning names they were called into their self-image. To mask this discomfort, particularly with peers, the adolescent may express statements of bravado ("I don't care what you think"), backing up a statement of not caring what others think by acting that way.

To parent against this emotional vulnerability, you need to respect the adolescent's efforts at transformation, taking them seriously, showing interest in them, and not dismissing or correcting them in a degrading way. *Treating trial differences with ridicule, with sarcasm, with negative humor, raises the risk of injuring fragile self-esteem with humiliation. The adolescent attempts to escape painful embarrassment at home by communicating with you less.*

What not to say: "Do you call that noise music?"
What to say: "Tell me about the group you are listening to."

PHASE THREE: THE DEPARTURE INTO INDEPENDENCE

With the expression of autonomous differences, the young person, through words and actions, signifies that the departure into independence, usually during the last years of high school, has begun. Now plans and preparations and the first steps toward living more independently are underway. "I'm ready to go!" declares the adolescent, soon discovering that he or she is really not, because some part of the young person doesn't want to leave. It will be many years before the adult child develops a confident independence, a living place as historically powerful as home, and a set of caring relationships as meaningful as family. Out of this awareness, the young person, departing into independence, confronts the emotional vulnerability of loss.

A desire to hold on can grip the young person the closer he gets to letting go, and scary questions come to mind. Once gone, will he or she be missed? Having left, will he or she now be left out of family life? Will no longer being a daily presence mean being forgotten? In response to this last question, the young person may take steps to secure the place that is being left behind. "Just 'cause I'm not there, you leave my room alone!" And belongings may be stored at home for years to show that one still belongs.

Preserving one's room, storing one's stuff, coming by for meals, and calling if away (why the first year off at college can be so expensive), are all ways to stay connected when living separately from family. Fear of loss of place in home and family can create enormous insecurity. "Suppose I go so far away I can't return? Then if I get in trouble, I'll have no safety net to fall back on, no home to come home to!"

If you treat your teenager's departure into independence as a surrender of all rights to residency at home, as "out of home, out of family," you increase the young person's social dependence on peers at a time when insecurity and various forms of excess are destabilizing many young people's lives. During the departure into independence, fear of loss of place at home can drive a teenager into dependence on companions who do not serve them well and can even do them harm.

> *What not to say:* "Now you're out of here and on your own!"
> *What to say:* "For as long as we have a home, you will always
>   have a welcome place to stay should you want to visit or
>   should temporary need or want arise."

It is important to parent against the vulnerabilities built into the phases of the larger adolescent process:

- To father against *loneliness,* focus on *inclusion,* not exclusion.
- To father against *self-consciousness,* focus on *respect,* not ridicule.
- To father against *loss,* focus on still *belonging,* not being cut off.

Your job as a father is to understand normal adolescent growth. You must develop and maintain realistic expectations of the process so that unrealistic expectations do not put you at risk of overreactions, unnecessarily inflaming ordinary encounters with your teenager. You must respect the emotional vulnerabilities of adolescence so that you do not push your teenager further away when growth is already creating distance between you.

You must not take unwelcome changes personally lest by acting offended you provoke secondary conflict that gets in the way of dealing with the primary issue at hand. Your teenager is not out to get you. Inconsiderate, yes. Unmindful, yes. But calculated, no. Your son or daughter is too preoccupied with personal growth to spend much time thinking of "getting" anyone, particularly a dad.

Each of the three phases of adolescence can feel threatening, the young person often needing courage to keep growing forward. The separation from childhood carries the threat: "Suppose I pull so far away that you abandon me?" The redefinition of identity carries the threat: "Suppose I become so different you reject me?" The departure into independence carries the threat: "Suppose I leave and you won't want me back?" It is one job of a father to reduce these threats by promising to stay connected. "I will never abandon you. I will always accept you. I will always welcome you back."

MISTAKE-BASED EDUCATION

Finally, no matter how frustrated you get with your teenager, take the time to normalize expectations about performance by acknowledging the human frailty all of us share. Try saying something like this after you've worked through his or her latest lapse in judgment.

"You know, this is just how learning in life works—when you're growing up and when you're a grown-up, too, because we keep growing up all our lives. Trial and error, that's how it works for everyone; learning after the fact from our mistakes is the most painful education of all. All we can do is try our best, keep trying when the going gets hard, learn doing right from doing wrong, credit ourselves for what works out well, and accept that a mixed performance is the best we can ever achieve. So you need to know that I may not have made your mistakes growing up, but I sure have made a bunch of my own, and I'll make some more before I'm through."

It is very hard for teenagers to discuss learning from poor choices with a father who acts like he has lived error-free. The admission of frailty humanizes a father for teenagers and makes him accessible, while the denial of frailty only idealizes the man and makes him hard to talk to. Admitting mistakes, disclosing an imperfect past, apologizing for misconduct, and making honest efforts to amend wrongdoing all go a long way toward creating an approachable father to whom teenagers can turn when unwise choices lead to unhappy consequences.

If he feels like it, a father can even post, say on the refrigerator door, the following principles of mistake-based education to provide some perspective on life.

- Everybody makes mistakes.

- A mistake is a choice people would make differently if they could it do over again.
- People don't makes mistakes because they want to; they make mistakes because they didn't know any better or didn't think more clearly at the time.
- All mistakes are costly, but they can be worth the expense if they are used to inform and instruct.
- A bad mistake can teach a good lesson.
- Making a mistake is not a failing; not learning from a mistake is a failing.
- It is ignorant to make a mistake; but it is stupid to repeat a mistake.
- Sometimes people have to repeat the same mistake a number of times when there is something hard they don't want to learn, before they finally stop acting stupid and wise up.
- The smartest people are not those who never make mistakes, but those who use mistakes to make better choices the next time around.
- The stupidest people are those who are unable or unwilling to admit mistakes.

The three phases described in this chapter provide a large framework for understanding adolescence. Use the next four chapters for a further examination of how the process typically unfolds across four more specific stages of growth. Hopefully, these descriptions will further clarify changes to expect in your adolescent, and common concerns and choices that they create for a father.

CHAPTER FIVE

FATHERING IN EARLY ADOLESCENCE (AGES 9–13)

This chapter begins describing the four-stage model for understanding and anticipating adolescent growth that I have developed from over 20 years of counseling experience with parents and teenagers. This model is under constant revision as young people and their parents keep teaching me more about the complexities of growing up and the perplexities of being a parent. My approach is as much about the psychology of being a parent as it is about the psychology of being an adolescent because it is managing the relationship between parent and teenager that is the focus of most of the counseling I do.

Since fathers tend to be more comfortable defining their role as a performance parent, chapters 5–8 describe salient stands a man can take in response to common problems that often arise during these four stages of adolescent growth:

- Early adolescence (ages 9–13), and the change for the worse;
- Mid-adolescence (ages 13–15), and the fight for more freedom;

- Late adolescence (ages 15–18), and the desire to act more grown up;
- Trial independence (ages 18–23), and the challenge of living on one's own.

In each stage of the way, I try to clarify the father's challenge and suggest actions he can take, what he can *do* or *say,* to support his son or daughter gathering more power of responsibility, always the goal of constructive growth. Often, these stands are unpopular with the adolescent, which is why some fathers prefer not to take them. However, to hang in there and stay connected with your adolescent, it is better to be counted on and counted in, than discounted and counted out.

Fathering an adolescent is not for the faint of heart. It can be unrewarding work because teenagers are often not complimentary of your efforts, particularly when some instructive or corrective discipline from you is in order. At least at the time, they may complain about how you are too arbitrary in your restrictions, too unfair in your sanctions, too out of touch, or too removed to really care. And yet, in counseling, where teenagers confide in me what they would never share with their parents, I often hear expressions of grudging appreciation for the father who is persistent, who will have his say, who will require responsibility, and who will listen and stay involved. "I don't like the way my dad keeps after me and takes me on, but at least I know he's trying to be part of my life and that he cares."

So as we begin the journey through adolescence, remember your goal: to be a *connected father* at every stage of the way.

ADOLESCENCE AND PUBERTY

Early adolescence begins with the separation from childhood, as your son or daughter starts to reject being defined and treated as a child. When this change occurs, you will begin to experience less closeness in the relationship than you knew before. You may find the early adolescent less open and less confiding, less welcoming of physical touch and demonstrations of affection, and less interested in continuing the old activities you used to do together. Now the adolescent journey to young manhood and young womanhood is underway, often accompanied by another journey, puberty, which is *not* the same.

Adolescence is mediated by personal choice as the young person experiments with sufficient life experience and struggles to learn sufficient responsibility to finally claim adult identity, adult independence, and adult status. It is primarily a process of psychological and social development. Starting around ages 9 to 13, it seems to take around 10 to 12 years. *Puberty* is mediated by the release of hormones that trigger physiological changes resulting in the young person becoming capable of sexual reproduction, in the process undergoing significant other bodily changes as well. Much of adolescent development and the direction it takes is a matter of choices the young person makes. Puberty is *not* a matter of choice, which is what causes adolescents undergoing pubescent change to feel so helpless. Like it or not, they have to learn to accept and play the physical hand their puberty deals them.

Puberty definitely affects your child's adolescent passage. Commonly beginning during the early adolescent years (ages 9 to 13) and sometimes lasting into the late adolescent years (ages 15 to 18), puberty varies widely between individuals. Everyone must go through it in their own individual way, at their own pace, finally catching up with everyone else in sexual maturity.

Steinberg and Levine, in *You & Your Adolescent* (1990), describe the confusion of the process well. "Some young people race through puberty in a year and a half, while others take five or six years to mature. This means that one teenager may complete puberty before another the same age begins. Best friends may look and feel worlds apart. As if this were not enough, the outcome of puberty is uncertain. Some young women develop large breasts and others small; some men have long penises and others short. . . . Adults know that bodies come in all shapes and sizes. . . . Young adolescents know no such thing. Finally, puberty follows an independent timetable, which bears little relation to other aspects of maturation. A girl may look like a woman long before she feels like one inside. A boy may be mature in almost every way but still look like a child."

In response to self-consciousness about physical alterations that puberty is inflicting (perhaps body odor, pimples, changing shape), a father needs to be sensitive, understanding, and patient with his adolescent and the unhappy moods that come from disliking how one looks. In addition, if you and your wife have not already done so, explain puberty, why it happens, and what changes it brings, so your son or daughter has some perspective on the process. And be mindful: Adolescence can begin before the onset of puberty; but when puberty begins it always intensifies adolescent change.

THE NEGATIVE ATTITUDE

Usually between the ages of 9 and 13, the separation from childhood begins as your little boy or girl's search for more worldly experience and a more grown-up identity gets under way. In the process, old boundaries of dependency and definition must be broken to open up new freedom for independent and individual growth.

The opening salvo of early adolescence is the negative attitude, or the birth of the "bad attitude," as parents more commonly call it. What happened to the child who was full of positive energy all the time and a pleasure to live with? Now a turn for the worse seems to have taken place. It's like someone pulls the plug on the young person and all his positive energy drains away, negative energy rising in its place. He now enters a phase that one father described as "developmental lumphood." All the early adolescent seems to want to do is lay around and complain about having nothing to do. Initiative in pursuing any interest seems to have drained away. Separating from childhood, he knows that he no longer wants to do what as a child he enjoyed doing, but he doesn't yet know how to replace the loss. He literally doesn't know what to do with himself. When it comes to positive motivation and direction, he's riding on empty, so negative motivation will have to do. All of a sudden, it's like having a critic in the family. He's critical of positive suggestions, of family activities, of other members of the family, and—what parents often don't see—critical of himself: "I hate being treated as a child!" Rejecting the child he was, rejecting himself, and angry at that rejection, he turns anger at self-rejection into criticism of those around him. What can particularly attract his anger are parental demands and limits, rules and restraints that now stand in the way of the increased freedom he wants. So a sense of grievance, a chip on the shoulder, develops: "What gives you the right to tell me what I can and cannot do? You're not the boss of the world!" Yet parents *are* the bosses of his world, and now he doesn't like it. As a child, he didn't mind their authority that much, but as an early adolescent wanting more room for independence, but not yet knowing how to achieve this objective, he resents their directions and restraints.

The onset of the "bad attitude" begins during early adolescence because people do not change unless they are dissatisfied with who and how they are. And the early adolescent is dissatisfied with his social role and status. Although puberty can be occurring at this time, from working with young people I believe the motivation to begin adolescence is largely independent of this hormonal change.

This is the age when a dad sees his son's capable body in a state of chronic inactivity, notices household tasks that could use doing, and wants to put the two together. But when he makes this suggestion, his son just gets angry: "Oh, leave me alone, you don't understand, I'm too tired!" Tired of what?, wonders the man. So what should the father do? Calling on his performance ethic, the dad needs to respond: "I know you don't feel like getting up, but you need to because I need your help." It is better for the boy to do something he doesn't like and have some involvement with his father, and sense of competence from accomplishing a task, than to let lack of purpose and inactivity lead him into a protracted state of boredom.

Protracted boredom is dangerous for the early adolescent because it only increases discomfort at this aimless stage of growth, adding pain as well, since boredom is rooted in loneliness. Boredom means the young person has no good way to connect to self, others, or the world. This is why "I don't know what to do with myself!" is a cry of pain from being caught in the early adolescent squeeze of wanting what he hates—inactivity. When it becomes intolerable, loneliness from boredom can create a dangerous staging area for impulse, where temptation to do something—anything an equally bored peer might suggest—can seem better than just sitting around.

Remember: This is the age of early experimentation with risk taking, when many young people try substances (cigarettes, alcohol, vapors from solvents) as an adventurous alternative to feeling bored, as an escape from loneliness. Your job as a father during their early adolescence is to keep your children sufficiently busy, challenged, and involved, so they do not fall prey to the temptations of impulse.

This is also the age when, to differentiate herself from the child she was, an early adolescent will reject previous activities that are actually still major sources of pleasure and self-esteem. "I'm too old to keep doing soccer. That was for when I was just a kid! I want to quit the team. I don't want to play anymore!" As the father who has coached the girl's team for three years, you know your daughter enjoys the camaraderie, the competition, and the competence she has developed. You also understand where this early adolescent desire to disconnect from the past is coming from: She wants to throw away "childish" activities—activities she misses and still enjoys—to show she is no longer "a child." She wants to disconnect from what she cares about.

So you test the waters of her resistance. She says she doesn't want to go to practice today. After hearing her arguments you still insist she go. She sullenly consents, letting your insistence overcome her resistance, and then she has a good time.

At this contrary age, she has satisfied two opposing objectives, getting what she wants both ways. First, she has gotten to save face by protesting. And second, since you (not her) are responsible for her attending, now she can enjoy the pleasure she would otherwise, out of obligation to adolescent change, have given up. So you've struck the first of many exhausting, and bewildering, early adolescent compromises in which she objects (to what you want her to do and why), you insist (on her doing it anyway), and she grudgingly consents (now free to have fun doing what she blames on you). When your daughter is asked why she still plays soccer by a friend who quit the team, she now has an acceptable explanation: "My dad makes me go!"

But suppose her resistance hardens? "I hate soccer! I'm tired of soccer! I want to quit!" Now you play for delay. "I'll consider your desire after the end of the season. If you still feel this strongly, we will talk about it then." And if she's still resolved to quit at the end of the season, you agree with a condition. " I am willing to let you quit soccer as long you substitute another sport in its place" (and you give her several choices). As her dad, you know that being physically active in a sport contributes to her self-esteem, so while you are flexible about what sport she chooses, you are firm that playing some sport at this time will continue to be part of her athletic life.

And don't waste time trying to change the early adolescent's negative beliefs:

- "Life is unfair."
- "I shouldn't have to do what I don't want to."
- "Work is not worth doing."
- "Rules are for other people, not for me."
- "No one should have the right to boss me around."

Don't argue to try and change the young person's mind. Just respectfully disagree, state what you believe, and push for what you want. This negativity marks the entry into early adolescence, and it sets the stage for the active and passive resistance that follows.

REBELLION

The name for this resistance is *rebellion*. People do not rebel without just cause, and now the negative attitude has given the adolescent adequate grievance. Resentment at "over-protective" restriction and "unfair" treatment by parents is now used to justify objecting to their demands. Rebellion is not primarily against parents. It is actually directed against the old compliant and dependent definition of being a child. *Early adolescent rebellion is about opposition against old self-definition, acted out against parents for transformation's sake.*

Rebellion takes two forms in early adolescence: passive and active resistance. *Active resistance* has to do with debate and disobedience. *Passive resistance* has to do with procrastination and delay. The more strong-willed your child, the more of each type of resistance you will likely receive. Ultimately, both kinds of resistance serve the same growth need: to help the adolescent gather the power to change.

And resistance works. To some degree, on some occasions, parents will be too distracted or too tired to follow up on a demand. They will allow the adolescent's resistance to back them off for some period of time, or entirely. At least, resistance can delay demand; at most, it can deny it. In either case, "more freedom" is the power gained. By actively resisting, the early adolescent expresses more disagreement and complaints about parental demands, questions the rightness of rules and the parental right to make rules, and endlessly argues about everything. "It's like training a trial attorney," one father (an attorney himself) complained, weary of this unremitting verbal challenge to his authority. But he had unwittingly honed his daughter's debate skills—from arguing with him so often and so hard she had learned to argue well. If he really didn't want to train a debater, he should simply have taken stands and not argued back.

On the other hand, by passively resisting, the early adolescent will put off obligations and requests until it takes repeated reminders for the young person to do what she was asked, supposed, or told to do. Getting help, getting information, getting a chore started or finished are now all done on *teenager time*. "I will, in a minute!" she promises. But by now, her dad knows that a teenage minute can drag on for hours. "Now!" he commands in irritation, after the umpteenth request. "Well, you don't have to get upset about it!" retorts the teenager, and finally does as asked (for example, does the dishes), but not completely (doesn't use soap). And the father feels like he's back to square one.

What's going on? It's a compromise called delay. It's like the adolescent is saying, "You can tell me what and I'll tell you when. When I get enough 'when,' I'll do what you want—partly." So after repeated requests her backpack is removed from the living room, but remnants of her snacking still remain. It takes power of parental insistence (supervision) to wear this resistance down: "I will keep after you and after you and after you until you do what I asked."

Supervision is one important way a father can stay connected to his passively resistant early adolescent. By doing so he demonstrates that when he requests something important, he will invest whatever energy it takes, for however long it takes, to get it to happen. Supervision is nagging. Nagging is the drudgework of parenting. But nagging is honorable work. It needs to be done. A father uses the relentless power of his insistence to wear teenager resistance down. In counseling I ask the stubborn 12-year-old why she finally did her chores after so much delay, and her answer is testimony to the power of parental supervision. "Because I got tired of my dad nagging and wanted to get him off my case!"

It takes a strong father to successfully cope with passive, early adolescent resistance. Here's a blue ribbon example from a father who demonstrates how it's done.

"She just took a shower and there they are where she always leaves them: wet towels on the bathroom floor. 'Would you please hang up the towels?' I ask. 'Sure,' she cheerfully replies. And I wait for what I know is coming next. 'In a minute.' I mean it's not like I haven't been through this torment before—like about a million times. So I wait an hour and check the bathroom and everything's okay. No one has disturbed the towels. They're still resting nicely, and probably so is she. So I poke my head into her room and remind her: 'The towels, you said you'd hang up the towels.' And now she looks at me and shakes her head. 'I wish you'd make up your mind,' she says as if the problem is all me. 'I'm doing my homework. You're always after me to do my homework. Can I do my homework?' Don't ask me how she does it, but now I'm feeling on the defensive. 'After you get your homework done you'll pick them up?' She just wearily nods her head like I'm some kind of idiot and doesn't know how she puts up with me. 'Yes! Yes! Yes! Will you let me get back to work?'

Now I feel like I'm imposing so I leave. Two hours later the towels are still there, and I find her watching TV. Now I have her dead to rights. This is indefensible. 'If you have time to watch TV, you have time to pick up towels.' She gives me this pained look. 'Once a week. Once a week I get to watch my favorite show. Is that asking too much? Once a week? The only one I care to see. I've done my homework. Now can I watch my program? As soon as it's over, I'll get the towels.' Well, she did get her homework done. 'Okay,' I say, 'but right after it's over, the towels. No more excuses.' She nods agreement and impatiently dismisses me with a wave of her hand. An hour and half later I can't believe it. Why can't I believe it? Would my eyes lie? The towels haven't been touched. I storm off to her room. Her light is out. 'The towels!' I yell into the dark. 'What? What's the matter?' a groggy voice asks as though I'd woken her up. I stand my ground. 'The towels!' I repeat. Silence. 'You woke me up to talk about towels?' she asks, implying that if something is wrong it's not with her. 'You're always after me to get in bed on time, to get enough sleep, and now you wake me up for this? For towels? Can't I get them in the morning? I'm tired too!'

'You promise,' I ask. 'I promise,' she says. 'Good night.' And now it's next morning and she's about to leave for the bus to school when I notice the towels from last night have been joined by more towels from this morning's shower. 'THE TOWELS!' I scream as though I'd been betrayed, which is how I feel. 'YOU PICK UP THOSE TOWELS NOW!' You should have seen the look of disbelief on her face. 'You want me to miss the bus? You want me to be late for school? For towels? Which is more important: towels or school?' And for once in my fathering life, once for sure, I made the right decision. 'School? The heck with school! YOU PICK UP THE TOWELS!'"

It's not a lot of fun to do, but it's worth the exhausting effort. A father who invests in supervision of early adolescents to accomplish household membership requirements like doing chores and picking up definitely keeps his teenagers tied into family. "Any time I try to get out of work at home, I get my dad coming after me."

Just as more frequent supervision at home is required to get household cooperation from your early adolescent, supervision of homework and even classroom behavior may be required for a father to support academic performance at school. Loss of academic motivation in early adolescence is not a problem to be solved so much as a reality to be worked with. You must help a disinterested, distracted, and disaffected young person still process the work assigned at school. Usually, it's not so much a matter of your early adolescent not wanting to do well. He just doesn't want to do the work required to do well. Getting out of homework is how this resistance is most commonly expressed.

Consider the following scenario. "Any homework tonight?" asks the father. "No," blithely replied his 13-year-old son. "No homework tonight! I got it done at school." And the father trusts this explanation, given repeatedly over a number of weeks, until a progress report from school arrives in the mail warning of failing grades due to missed assignments. What's happening? His son who took care of homework in the sixth grade, in seventh is choosing not to get it done. Why? The answer is the demotivating effect of early adolescence and the school achievement drop that often occurs at this time. The young person rebels against self-interest (maintaining school performance) to assert opposition to the system (declaring independence of established authority), and then lies about what is going on (to conceal misbehavior from parents).

At first the father thinks punishment might be the answer. "Because you didn't do your homework and lied to us about it, you're grounded for the next month! And we'll keep grounding you every time we find out homework is not being done!" Of course, soon the father realizes the error of his corrective way. Now he has turned a performance issue into a power issue that only challenges his son to go down in flames of failure to show his dad who is really in charge of homework decisions. Even worse, the father has made it sound like completing homework is an option—choose not to do it and punishment follows—so the boy chooses punishment, which feels worth the crime.

Now the father realizes that he must treat homework, like chores, as unavoidable obligations. They are a given. They *will* be done. By using supervision, not punishment, the father makes this certainty so. Knowing that his more independent early adolescent now wants his dad to stay away from school because the presence of parents is a social embarrassment with peers, the father makes his son an offer the young man cannot refuse. "Unless you take care of business at school, I will show up and help you do so. If you lie about homework, you and I will meet TOGETHER with the teacher, when you will have a chance to explain why you said homework was done when it wasn't, and how you plan to get it done hereafter. If you still can't manage to bring it home or turn it in, I will meet you at the end of your last class and TOGETHER we shall walk the halls and visit classrooms to pick all assignments up. And if you do it, but don't turn it in, I will accompany you to school in the morning and TOGETHER we shall walk the halls so you can deliver it to your teachers. And as far as not paying attention or acting out in class, if that is not corrected, I will come into your class and we will sit TOGETHER to make sure you are doing what the teacher asks." Hearing his father's declaration, the boy is in shock. "You can't do that! All my friends will make fun of me!" To which the father replies, "I am not doing this to embarrass you. I do not want to do this, but I am willing to do this to help you accomplish the work to get the grades that show how you are capable of performing. I am doing this *for* you, not against you. I am on your side, the one that supports doing well in school to give you additional cause to feel good about yourself. I would not be a responsible parent, I would not be doing you any favors, by letting you fail to do your work."

Supervise your adolescent's performance at school. Explain what you are doing to your adolescent this way: "Part of my job as your father is to help you do your job at school. I want to help you learn to work at what you may not always like, to help you develop the will to work, to help you work up to your capacity, and to help you make choices now that keep opportunities open in the years ahead." Part of your connection to your early adolescent is to represent future considerations to a young person who has a very hard time seeing beyond "now." Part of your job is also to keep a watchful eye out for early experimentation.

EARLY EXPERIMENTATION

With new freedom gained from rebellion, the early adolescent now has room to experiment with image and appearance, new and different friends, more risk taking, and the forbidden, and tests limits to see what he can get away with. Where the negative attitude has to do with gathering the motivation to change, and rebellion has to do with gathering the power to change, early experimentation has to do with gathering the older experience to change. Leaving childhood behind and looking out at the grown-up world, the young person is filled with fear and curiosity that combine to create a sense of drama, adventure, and excitement. A sense of daring is in the early adolescent air, daring to experience what lays beyond the prohibitions that parents and other social authorities have prescribed.

"Which rules are firm and which are not?" That is the question the early adolescent wants to answer. The only way to find out is to do some limit testing to see what she can get away with. Where no adverse consequence occurs, that is a place where more social freedom is apparently allowed. Keep in mind, the more illicit freedom an early adolescent is permitted to get away with, the more unmindful of social rules she becomes. So it becomes the father's salient role, should he choose to accept it, to represent the larger social authority within the context of family life. His son or daughter must confront him when, out in the world, they cross over boundaries of prohibited behavior.

This is the age when experimentation, not just with substances but with rule breaking—for example, committing pranks, vandalizing, and shoplifting—usually begins.

For a father who has an adolescent history of serious troublemaking, it can be tempting to write this early experimentation off as innocent mischief, but such permissiveness is not a good idea. Better to close the loop of responsibility by insisting his early adolescent face the consequences of her actions. Better for the young person to encounter the victim and confess ("I played the harmful joke" or "I defaced your property"), hear the victim's emotional response to what happened, clean up any damages done, and make some kind of restitution. Let these early violations go, and more serious and dangerous limit testing and rule breaking are likely to follow.

Consider a case of shoplifting. One weekend afternoon a father picks up the phone to hear the tear-filled voice of his 12-year-old daughter calling him to be picked up right away. "Where are you?" he asks, alarmed. "I thought you were at your friend's." "I was. But now I'm at the police department," she manages to blurt out. "Why are you there?" he asks, relieved she is in a safe place. "We were caught shoplifting and the police were called and took us in. Will you come and pick me up right away? Please!" "Sure," agrees her father, and then waits about an hour and a half, giving his daughter some time to let her offense and incarceration sink in. Finally arriving, he gets the details of what happened and signs his daughter out.

In the car she starts to relax until she notices they are not driving directly home. "Hey! Where are we going?" "To the store where you were caught stealing. To meet with the manager and hear what it was like for him to be stolen from, to say something in response, and to figure out whatever restitution needs to be made." "But I don't want go back there! I don't want to talk to the manager!" "Choices have consequences," explains her father, "and confronting the consequences of your actions, in this case the victim of what you did, is how you learn to take responsibility."

In the company of her friend, his daughter stole not to get something she particularly wanted, but to engage in risk taking to see what she could get away with. Her father's actions backed up the social prohibition she broke and put her on notice that he is prepared to continue to act for her good, against what she likes, should she attempt something like this again.

One diagnostic tool a father can use at this age to assess trouble spots ahead are extreme aversion statements.

- "I hate the idea of using drugs!"
- "I can't stand her (him)!"
- "I'd never do that!"

Beware aversion conversions. Early adolescents often speak in extreme terms to deny strong feelings of attraction or interest. Finally, early adolescence is a good time for you to begin training your son or daughter in impulse management. "Low self control is . . . a risk factor for a broad range of personal and interpersonal problems." (See Tangney, Baumeister, and Boone in *Journal of Personality,* vol. 72, no. 2, April 2004.) One practical way to train your son or daughter to exercise self-control is to have them systematically start saving some money from odd jobs, gifts, and allowance. I have found in counseling that whether an adolescent is a spender or saver of money is often connected to self-control. Young spenders seem to be ruled by temptation, young savers more capable of self-restraint. So I say to parents: "Teaching your early adolescents to save is literally and figuratively 'putting money in the bank' because they learn to goal set, think of the future, plan for later, delay gratification, tolerate self-denial, and exercise patience."

A father's job in early adolescence is to keep the young person involved in constructive activities when the negative attitude is causing disengagement, to use supervision to wear down resistance from rebellion, and to cause the young person to take responsibility for early experimentation when limit testing has gone out of bounds.

CHAPTER SIX

FATHERING IN MID-ADOLESCENCE (AGES 13–15)

Mid-adolescence is the proving ground for many fathers. Proving what? Proving that they are really committed to hanging in there and staying connected to their teenager during what is often the stormiest of the four adolescent stages. Fail to maintain a salient presence here and you may become marginalized during the two stages to follow—you risk being relegated to the parenting sidelines when your guidance would help during late adolescence, and avoided when your maturity is needed during trial independence.

Adolescence, as has been well noted, is about freedom for self-determination. "The adolescent feels driven to be independent. He has to make his own decisions, choose his own friends, and determine his own future. There is a real, powerful drive for emancipation and independence." (See Teicher in *California Medicine,* vol. 85, no. 3, September 1956.) The older the adolescent gets, the more self-determined he wants to be, hence the mid-adolescent pushes harder for this freedom than the early adolescent.

Mid-adolescence is so trying for fathers because it is often when the hardest push against parental constraints occurs. In early adolescence, restriction on personal freedom is primarily a theoretical issue for the young person to argue about, establishing a grievance against the unfairness of parents in order to justify actively and passively resisting their authority. "What gives you the right to tell me what I can and cannot do?"

Come mid-adolescence, however, the young person really wants to be out in the world, exploring, experiencing, and experimenting in the company of friends who are more important than ever before, and (according to your child) who all have parents who allow more running room than you do. The push in mid-adolescence is for more freedom than is often safe, a push made stronger by companions who are all feeling more restless and reckless, none of whom are confident enough to try out acting older alone. At this stage, parental cautions are discounted as exaggerated worries: "You're being overprotective!" Teenage assurance pretends to worldly understanding the teen does not actually possess: "I know all about it!" Risk taking is protected by denial: "Nothing bad is going to happen to me!"

During the mid-adolescent push, it is worthwhile to organize all the supplemental adult influence in the teenager's life you can. A team coach, a scout leader, a special activity instructor, a youth group minister, extended family members that matter, a beloved family friend, a camp counselor, a tutor, a trusted parent of a teenage peer: Socially tie your adolescent in to all the significant adults that the young person values.

If faith so inclines you, encourage your teenager to attend your church youth group. Often run by a leader who teenagers can comfortably talk to, these regular gathering places can provide a healthy home away from home—a place where social cliques are not as influential as at school, where support and recreation can be enjoyed, service activities and mission trips experienced, and leadership learned. Summer camps can also be anchoring experiences, familiar places to which a young person returns year after year, first as camper, then as counselor-in-training, then as counselor, that offer meaningful adult connections in the adolescent's life. As father, part of your job can be fostering and supporting positive adult relationships that can successfully compete with those offered by peers.

Another part is keeping up with the changes in your mid-adolescent's life. Speech patterns is a good place to start because you likely will notice a difference in how your teenager talks. Conversation is not as direct as it used to be, more frequently spoken in a kind of code that you must crack. Why the change? To create misunderstanding that may, in a given situation, create some protection from accountability.

Here's a partial lexicon.

"I can't help it" can mean
"I won't stop it."

"I forgot" can mean
"I chose not to remember."

"You don't trust me" can mean
"You don't believe my story."

"You worry too much" can mean
"Your suspicions are interfering with my plans."

"I don't know" can mean
"I don't want to tell what I know."

"I hate you" can mean
"I am extremely angry you won't let me."

"I don't care" can mean
"I care too much to show how much I care."

"You wouldn't understand" can mean
"I don't want you to understand."

"I'll tell you whatever you want to know" can mean
"I won't tell more than you think to ask for."

"You're not listening" can mean
"You're not agreeing with what I said."

"You don't love me" can mean
"You won't let me do what I want."

One of your new jobs as a father in mid-adolescence is learning to hear beyond the code in which your son or daughter now often speaks so you can connect to what he or she really means. Thus informed, you can call her on the untruth in her communication. For example, told by your daughter that you do not love her after you deny a request, you can set the record straight. "As you really know, just because I won't let you do what you want, doesn't mean I don't love you. In fact, it means I love you enough to make a decision for your best interests that you do not like."

Particularly during mid-adolescence, fathering is not a popularity contest. And as teenagers this age frequently report in counseling, the parenting decisions most disliked have to do with setting limits on freedoms that the teen now highly prizes and pushes hard to get. Hence limit setter is a thankless and valuable role to play because it firmly anchors the dad as a socially restraining presence to be reckoned with during this impetuous and expansive period. There are two specific arenas of activity where by taking specific limit-setting positions, a father can symbolically communicate that he intends to be involved in the conduct of his teenager's life. The first arena is the messy room: How messy is it allowed to get? The second is the Internet: What limits will you set within this vast world of information and interaction?

THE MESSY ROOM

In many ways, the "messy room" is emblematic of the mid-adolescent age. Usually beginning in early adolescence because of personal disorganization brought on by more growth change than the young person can easily keep up with; by mid-adolescence this state of spatial disarray has grown to assume anarchic value. It represents the freedom to live at home on the teen's own personal terms.

"It's my room! ", is a typical response from the mid-adolescent. "I should be free to live in it any way I want!" In early adolescence, the messy room often reflects personal disorganization brought about when the ordered simplicity of childhood is left behind. In mid-adolescence, however, a specific disagreement over order becomes a symbolic struggle over who's in charge of setting limits. To the father, the messy room can feel like a deliberate challenge to domestic order, which in fact it is. Further, because the father's home is a reflection and extension of himself, and often partly an outcome of his labor, he can end up feeling disrespected, personally trashed by the mess his daughter creates.

But when the dad weighs in for order, his mid-adolescent rises to a power issue worth contesting, and so commences the conflict of mess up vs. clean up that can unfold over many years, a battle in which she has a lot at symbolic stake. By asserting her right to a messy room, she is bringing up issues of independence, individuality, and opposition to parental rules.

- As a statement of independence, the teenager seems to say: "I should be able to live in my own space on my own terms!"
- As a statement of individuality, the child seems to say: "I have a right to whatever personal definition I so choose!"
- As a statement of opposition, the child seems to say: "I'm going to live my way, not your way!"

So, does the dad just ignore the messy room, accepting it as a natural byproduct of his daughter's more freedom-loving age? Does he adjust to what he doesn't like and then get angry with her for what he has tacitly allowed? No. Instead, he takes a salient stand. He declares his role as limit setter. "Although you can choose to mess up your room to your satisfaction, you need to know that two or three times a week, at a time convenient to me, it must be cleaned up to my satisfaction before you get to do whatever else you might be wanting to do." Then he votes with his relentless supervision to enforce this condition of family living.

To get her to conform to household order requirements, he commits to oversee her picking up and cleaning up. And this includes the rest of the home when her messiness spills over into other rooms. Expansive mid-adolescents are extremely territorial, taking over as much family space as they can get. Leaving belongings out and about to mark and claim additional space beyond their bedroom door creates a presence parents can often find intrusive and oppressive: "Her things are everywhere!" Half-eaten snacks, scattered laundry, dirty dishes, household arrangements out of place, borrowed objects not put back, are all markings that must be contained if the presence of the ever-expansive mid-adolescent is to be kept within tolerable parental limits. The larger living space also requires that the father patrol, engaging and connecting with his son or daughter at every picking up point.

His territorial supervision also has two larger messages to convey. First, he demonstrates that she must live on parental terms so long as she is dependent on parental care, and second, by keeping after her about this "small stuff," he implies he will be keeping after "big stuff" like obedience to major rules. Of course, if he has an extremely distractible teenager who has been diagnosed with an attention deficit, imposing spatial order is not only for the father's sake. It is also to benefit the son or daughter for whom personal disorganization only makes paying attention and concentrating that much harder to do. Simplicity creates fewer choices to manage than complexity. Order supports concentration; disorder creates distraction.

Returning to the argument between the mid-adolescent and her father over how to manage the messy room, now the daughter has a suggestion. "Just close the door and keep out and the mess won't bother you." He needs to decline her self-serving offer. Allow her mess to keep him and his supervision out and she may start using freedom from surveillance to start keeping things and conducting activities in the room that he does not want in his home or in her life. At the age of awakening curiosity about the grown-up world, such freedom can be abused— treated as license to explore and experiment with the forbidden.

After refusing to let her mess keep him out, the father is given a teenage ultimatum: "This is my room and you can't come in without my permission. I have a right to privacy!" To which declaration, the father answers "Yes" and "No." "Yes, I will knock before entering if the door is closed; but no, your privacy is not a right, it is a privilege. Use freedom of personal space within the limits of agreed-upon responsibility, and I will respect your privacy. Use privacy for purposes of doing or keeping what is forbidden, however, and that privilege is lost."

In general, at least by mid-adolescence, you might want to declare an "open door policy" when your teenager has friends over, the open door being the one to her bedroom, which is to remain ajar so long as she is entertaining friends in there. It's tempting for adolescents to exploit privacy for concealment. An open door policy keeps that temptation down. Just as he patrols time with friends, spending, driving, cell phone use, and the Internet in her life, her father patrols the limits of responsible bedroom use.

What the man may or may not tell his daughter is that now another right comes into play, his right to investigate if denied adequate information for understanding what is going wrong in her life and why. But this is not a simple right to assume. To respect or not respect the teenager's privacy? That is a troubling question for parents at this challenging stage. For many parents, exercising the right to investigate seems disrespectful and excessively intrusive. So consider what you would or would not do differently in the following example.

A father sees his daughter's grades suddenly plummet in the first year of high school because she's not turning in homework. He catches her in lies about her new friends, some of whom turn out to be older than she reported and not in school. There are instances of sneaking out. Strange phone calls come for her and the callers refuse to leave their names. Her physical appearance changes. She looks tired all the time and her mood becomes sullen and withdrawn. What's going on? When he asks her, he gets little response. So the father decides to go data gathering, to investigate. He starts by going through her room, only to discover notes, letters, and a diary outlining a double life he never suspected, this second life of early substance use putting her at significant risk. A further search of her online communications fills the dangerous picture out. Now he begins to make sense of what is going wrong.

The only thing he can't understand is why his daughter allowed incriminating evidence to be so easily found. The answer usually is that like most mid-adolescents, she is scared by all the freedom at her disposal. She is both liberated and frightened by the knowledge that her parents can't make her behave or stop her. Lacking the courage to tell them directly what is going on, but desperate for parents to know, she leaves evidence in plain sight in the hopes of being found out. Like many young people this age, it feels easier to get caught than to confess. It's also easier to explain to friends her sudden social restriction. "They snooped and busted me!" beats telling peers she volunteered to let her parents know. Having illicitly taken so much freedom that her life felt unsafe, this mid-adolescent is secretly glad to have parental help to get it back under control, and to have saved face in the process.

This is why mid-adolescence is the stage when parental prohibitions are ironically most effective, because your teenager knows

- that you can't control her or stop her,
- that you are running a home, not a prison,
- that her freedom of action is all fundamentally up to her,
- and that this is more freedom than she can comfortably handle.

So what she needs from you *are the protections of your prohibitions.* She needs to blame not doing, not going along with friends, on you: "I really want to, but my dad says I can't and would ground me forever if I did!" So in mid-adolescence list your prohibitions and in clear language make them known. She may object to your face, but she will file them away should she ever feel the need for their protective use.

THE INTERNET

But how can you protect your mid-adolescent from the Internet, a whole new world that you were never exposed to while growing up? Often, teenagers know more about this world and navigate it far more expertly than their fathers, who are playing catch-up in understanding a very marvelous and very dangerous electronic frontier. Because the teenager is more "worldly" in this new world than the man, a wise father will enlist the more sophisticated teenager as teacher and guide. This instructional role is gratifying for the teenager, who is recognized for possessing expertise the man lacks, and is valuable for the father, who has much to learn from his teenager's instruction.

"Estimates suggest that up to 90% or more youth between 12 and 18 have access to the Internet." (See Ybarra and Mitchell in *CyberPsychology & Behavior,* vol. 8, no. 5, 2005.) The Internet is the new playground, street corner, and all-purpose hangout. It's where you go to interact with people you know and meet people you don't. It's an infinite amusement center filled with all manner of make-believe. It is truly "a whole new world."

Now imagine what happens when you combine an expansive mid-adolescent with this world of endless informational, interactive, and entertainment possibilities. The question for you to consider is a very simple one, although the answer is extremely complex. "Where in the vast world of the Internet do you want, and do you not want, your teenager to go?"

You *must* stake out a position in this world (set acceptable boundaries) and you must attend to your teenager's Internet experience, offering adult commentary in response (providing mature perspective). You are not trying to change the young person's mind, but you are trying to broaden his or her understanding by adding your own. "I know you think chatting about yourself with strangers you don't actually meet is safe, but I do not and here is why." Many fathers find that keeping track of sites their mid-adolescents are visiting has both restraining and informative value. It keeps visitation within prescribed limits and provides a continual stream of talking points about the young person's interests at this time of life. Make sure your teenager understands: "There is nowhere you can go on the Internet I cannot follow because you always leave an electronic trail."

What kinds of trails might catch a dad's attention? Consider the father who notices that his 15-year-old son, the eldest of the four children, is visiting pornographic sites on the family computer. According to the Internet Safety Group (see www.NetSafe.org) "most adolescent boys will look at pornography in the course of their [teenage] lives." However, although the father isn't surprised, he does want to talk to his son about this behavior because it impacts not only the mid-adolescent but the family as well. Confronting the young man, the father is told: "I was just curious, that's all." But the father has data to the contrary. "According to my searches, you have visited these sites for over six months. So your interest is no longer just experimental, to see what sex is like for curiosity. Now your interest is recreational, to get enjoyment from stimulation. There is nothing wrong with the fact that you are curious and that sexual stimulation is now pleasurable. However, the Internet can open a doorway of information into this house, and there are certain kinds of sites, those that promote harmful influences like drug use, hate, violence, and gambling, that we want to keep our family free from. When you bring pornographic sex into the home via the Internet, you expose your brother and sisters to this material. I believe pornographic sex sites are harmful to them and to you because these pictures make it appear that sex is no big deal, when I believe it is. For what it's worth, here's my concern. Right now you are putting together your impressions of what relationships are about and have to offer, and how they should be treated, and pornography makes it seem like they are good for sex and nothing more. Further, these sites ignore the consequences of casual sex—from disease to pregnancy to sexual violence—making it seem that free and indiscriminate sex is safe, when casual sex between people can be dangerous. And, since most of the people who enjoy pornography are men, it is primarily created to portray women as wanting nothing more than to satisfy a man's sexual desires. In addition, by exploiting sex, pornography actually lessens the value of sex and relationships."

Obviously, this man's view does not have to match your own; however, as the father you do need to put pornography into the mature context of your own values and beliefs, because it's ultimately by informing your teen's beliefs that you will influence his behavior. The same applies for your daughter, with this addition. Although adolescent girls are less likely to seek out pornographic sites than boys, they are *more* likely to receive online sexual solicitations. According to the *U.S. Justice Department Youth Internet Safety Survey* (see Fact Sheet FS–200104) "one third of the surveyed youth who had received a sexual solicitation were male; two-thirds were female." And "In 67% of the incidents youth were at home." Tell your daughter to let you know if she receives sexual solicitations. You do not want her being targeted or victimized in this harassing way. You and her mother want to listen should she have questions to ask or feelings to share about disturbing online experiences.

Of course, if the issue becomes putting a stop to your son's persistent home use of the Internet for pornographic interest, despite parental directions to the contrary, this is very easy to do. All you have to do is turn the forbidden experience into an extensive talking point. You can say something like this. "Before you get to do anything else you want to do, you need to sit down with your mother and I to talk about what you have seen. We want you to specifically describe three acts you saw you think your younger brother and sisters are too young to see. We want you to tell us three responses you think the maker of the film wanted you to experience, three ideas about relationships the movies taught, and three risks in what you saw that the participants seemed to ignore." Communication can be the most unwelcome consequence of all.

If ever there was a mixed blessing, it is the Internet. It is a vast source of information (so you need to supervise this education), it is a vast opportunity for interaction (so you need to monitor those communications), and it is vast source of entertainment (so you need to make sure those escapes are not taking up too much time). For a connected father, mid-adolescence takes a lot of parental involvement.

WHEN THE GOING GETS TOUGH

During this period of newfound freedom, your mid-adolescent can put you under pressure, engage you in conflict, be absent without leave (AWOL), and sometimes lie to your face to get to have, to get to do, to get to go. At this age, should you have the temerity to deny permission, particularly permission you teen's other friends have been given, you may get desperation statements in response. "You've ruined my life!" "If you don't let me I'll never forgive you!" "I'll never do anything you ask me to do again!"

During mid-adolescence, emotion can speak with an extremely dire voice, so don't get caught in the moment and panic in response. Let the moment pass and the urgency will subside—until the next "must have" demand for freedom arises. On these extreme occasions, under no circumstances escalate your emotional response because you will only end up fueling the fire. You will be agreeing to play the parent/teenager interaction by mid-adolescent rules: The person who makes the most intense scene wins. And you will lose.

There are all manner of useful stands for a father to clarify and take at this age, defining expectations, terms, conditions, boundaries, limits, and standards to structure a safe and healthy passage through an impetuous period of growth. Of course, the teenager will challenge you with all argumentative and manipulative power at his disposal. He will try to pressure you to abandon a stand you know is right at a time when the desire for more worldly experience (which is healthy) exposes your son or daughter to more worldly danger (which can be destructive). The only part of your "No" the teenager doesn't understand is *why* he can't manage to somehow, some way, get you to relent.

Of all four stages of adolescence, mid-adolescence is the one where the most conflict typically arises. This is the time when a healthy teenager will push for all the freedom she can get as soon as she can get it, and when a healthy parent restrains that push within the limits of safety and responsibility. The ensuing conflict of interests unfolds throughout the rest of adolescence, but rarely as intensely as during this mid-adolescent time. Your job as father is to be full partner with your teenager during this ongoing dance of opposition so your restraining influence can be felt. Hang in there and it will. Back off and it will not.

Reflecting back on this hotly contested period of parenting years later, you will see that your influence in conflict was partly successful, and partly not. You received less cooperation than you ideally wanted, but your mid-adolescent gave more consent than she ideally wished. Compromise was how you learned to get along, in the process listening to what each other had to say. She lived mostly within your rules and restraints, and occasionally outside of them, just like you did with your parents. She told you some, but not all, about what was going on, just like you did with your parents. But you kept insisting on responsible behavior, demanding discussion of the risks of freedom, and taking protective stands, which she did not appreciate.

Mid-adolescence is when thankless parenting truly arrives. Your job is to slow down the rush for freedom with delay ("I want time to think about it"), with discussion ("We need to talk about it"), and with denial ("The answer's 'no' and this is why.") Sometimes you need to be a drag on your teenager to slow down the rush for worldly freedom. You need to set conditions to create a measure of safety, and you need to demonstrate that you will not back down from important issues.

Your teenager will exert pressure when you are standing in the way of what he wants or what he wants to do. By mid-adolescence the teenager has usually matured physically and emotionally, and he may be prepared to use these changes to pressure you into submission, using his larger size and intensity to bullying effect.

In a situation from my counseling, a son was denied permission to go out to a late night concert with an older crowd of friends he had made through sports. The young man, who was almost as large as his father, went to work to get his way. He crowded the man's personal space, got in his face, raised his voice, and loudly argued and gestured in an angry and threatening way, all to try and intimidate his father.

Counseling the dad about curtailing his son's aggressive efforts, I suggested that the man do the unexpected to discourage repetition of this bullying behavior. "How does your son predict you will behave under this pressure?" I asked. "Specifically what behaviors does he expect from you?" The dad thought for a moment and then gave me five: "He expects me to look alarmed, look away, step back, shut up, and try to put space between us." That's when we talked about violating the boy's prediction. In other words, the next time the son tried to pressure his dad to back off, this is what the father said he did. "I gave him a big smile, looked him in the eyes, stepped toward him so our noses almost touched. Then I put my hands on his shoulders and pulled him closer, kissed him on the cheek, and said 'I love you when you act like this.'" This was not the response the son predicted, and certainly not the one he wanted, so the teenager did not try that particular pressure tactic again. Having lost a single battle, however, did not mean the teenager had given up contesting freedom with his father.

THE DANCE OF CONFLICT

Conflict with the mid-adolescent can be confusing because by intentionally creating confusion in disagreement the teenager can sometimes get his way. How? The young person becomes a master of two tactics: *evasion* and *distraction*. Both tactics prevent a father from effectively engaging in conflict with his teenager. They get in the way of agreeing on a definition of what is going on and what needs to happen to resolve the problem. For the mid-adolescent, the point of engaging in conflict is to escape discussing the unwanted and doing the undesirable. Evasion and distraction are how this is commonly done.

Here is an example of how a determined father wrestles with words to pin his slippery mid-adolescent down.

The Father says:	The Teenager responds:
"You didn't turn in any homework this week." *(Specific issue)*	"I'm working much harder, like I promised. Why don't you ever give me credit for trying?" *(Abstract issue)*
"Three teachers I talked to said they asked you for your homework, that you said you'd turned it in, and that you never did." *(Accurate statement)*	"You always side with the teachers. You never side with me!" *(Extreme statement)*

"What are you going to do to get the overdue homework in?" *(Present focus)*	"All you do is bring up the past against me. I'll get it done if you'll just leave me alone!" *(Past or future focus)*
"Your job is to get the homework, do it, and turn it in when due." *(Expects responsibility)*	"It's not my fault if the teachers don't give me clear assignments." *(Makes excuses)*
"I want a plan for making up your homework." *(Declaration)*	"You don't care about my feelings. All you care about is school!" *(Manipulation)*
"I intend to keep talking to you about homework until it gets done." *(Sticking to the subject)*	"Where's supper? I'm hungry. Why can't we ever eat on time?" *(Changing the subject)*
"We will eat after we have agreed on getting in the missing work." *(Insisting on resolution)*	"All right! I'll do the extra work tonight and turn it in tomorrow!" *(Giving agreement)*

Conflict becomes like a dance of engagement and avoidance. Unless the father is determined to bring closure to those issues upon which the well-being of his teenager depends, he may find his influence eroding. Unable to resist arguing with the diversionary tactics the teenager raises, he will get sidetracked and be put on the defensive, unwittingly following the teenager everywhere but where the father wants the conversation to go.

Remember, when in conflict with your mid-adolescent, stick to your agenda by

- discussing specifics,
- making accurate statements,
- focusing on the present,
- assuming responsibility,
- declaring wants,
- sticking to the subject,
- reaching agreement,
- and insisting by example that your son do the same.

"AWOL"

Although sneaking out commonly begins in early adolescence after parents are supposed to be asleep, mid-adolescence is the age of *the end run,* becoming absent without parental leave (AWOL). For example, your teenager stays at a friend's house (where parents might be less vigilant and more lenient) to get away with freedom unavailable at home. The *single end run* refers to when your teenager spends the night over at a friend's house and both friends sneak out for a night on the town. The *double end run* refers to times when your son tells you he is going to stay at the friend's, the friend tells his parents he is going to stay with you, and now both are cleared to stay at neither place and so can use the night for adventure. As the father, assume responsibility for checking on all overnight arrangements.

The extreme version of this behavior is *going on a run,* when your teenager leaves without any notice or storms out of the house to take freedom you have either not permitted or have denied. This is fairly common behavior at this age, and although upsetting to many parents, it can be curtailed. Supervision in the form of pursuit is the most effective response. I've had fathers tell me how they have gone to the park, to the downtown drag, or to the older friend's apartment where their son (or daughter) is hanging out with friends, and put in a patient but persistent appearance until the young man accepts the invitation to return. Horrified that his father would be willing to track him down in this publicly embarrassing way in front of friends, the young man sullenly accompanies his dad home.

When a child goes on a "mid-adolescent run," taking freedom for freedom's sake, the father who is committed to parental pursuit and putting in an intrusive presence can provide a powerful deterrent to repetition.

THE POWER OF LYING

With this chapter it is time to revisit the topic of lying. Lying becomes increasingly common in mid-adolescence, when a father may begin to wonder: "Whatever happened to the truth?" His little girl or boy may not always have been honest, but teenagers are prone to lie both by commission (telling a deliberate falsehood) and by omission (not voluntarily disclosing what parents need to know). Your job as father is to hold your teenagers to truthful account during a time when they are less inclined to give you accurate or adequate information about what is really going on.

For example, just consider ten very common mid-adolescent lies.

1. "I already did it."
2. "I didn't do it."
3. "I was about to do it."
4. "I'll do it later."
5. "I promise."
6. "I didn't think you'd mind."
7. "I didn't know that's what you meant."
8. "I didn't think you were serious."
9. "It wasn't my fault."
10. "It was an accident."

Why do mid-adolescents tend to lie more? It is usually for freedom's sake—to delay compliance, to excuse noncompliance, to escape punishment for misbehavior, or to get to do what has been denied. To many teenagers at this age, lying seems to be the easy way out. But lying is deceptive: What seems simple at the moment proves complicated over time. The "easy way out" turns out to be personally costly, particularly for teenagers who get so deeply into lying that they have a hard time digging themselves out.

What these mid-adolescents discover is that lying hurts themselves most of all. They have more to remember—the reality that happened, the fiction they told, and the difference between the two. They find themselves living in fear of being found out and they feel out of control, as telling one lie necessitates more lies until they can't keep everything straight. As they protectively pull away from parents to lessen the chance of discovery, they put more distance between themselves and the people they love, and feel cut off and lonely as a result. As estrangement builds, they discover how the lies they tell isolate them in the family. No wonder they're relieved to be finally found out. Now honesty allows open communication once again.

If you become aware, after several weeks of evasive communication from your teenager, that they are trying to conceal something, you can make this sympathetic intervention: "It's hard to lie without experiencing pressure from the secrecy you keep. A lie hurts the liar even more than those to whom the lie is told because it's hard to live in hiding, particularly from those you love. To relieve your pressure, I'd like you to know I know you have been lying and that whenever you want to get the pressure off and get back on a relaxed and honest and open footing with me, I am ready to hear what you have to say."

As a guardian of the truth, a father needs to treat lying seriously. The quality of family life depends as much as anything on the quality of communication, and lying can erode that quality to devastating effect. There is no trust without truth. There is no intimacy without honesty. There is no safety without sincerity. And there is no such thing as a small lie because overlooking one lie only encourages the telling of another.

So, here are some steps you can take when your mid-adolescent lies.

1. Explain the high costs of lying so the teenager understands the risks that go with dishonesty.

2. Declare how it feels to be lied to so the teenager understands how loving relationships can be emotionally impacted by dishonesty.

3. Apply some symbolic reparation—a task the teenager must do that he or she would not ordinarily have to do—to work the offense off.

4. Insist on a full discussion about the lying—why it occurred, what the teenager is going to do to prevent further lying, and what the teenager may need from parents in order to make future truth telling feel safer to do.

5. Declare that lying in the family will always be treated as a serious offense.

6. Reinstate parental trust and the expectation that truth will be told in order to give the teenager a chance to resume a healthy and honest relationship. To do any less ("You'll have to earn my trust back") only encourages the teenager to keep lying ("Why tell the truth if I won't be believed?") and encourages the father to drive himself crazy ("I live in a state of constant distrust!"). This can be very hard, but it is necessary.

7. Most important, if you want your teenagers to tell the truth, be a truth teller yourself.

The father's job in mid-adolescence is to set responsible limits on freedom, to withstand manipulative pressure, to engage in constructive conflict, to pursue obedience to rules, and to insist on telling the truth, in order to create a firm parenting position for the two stages of adolescence to follow.

CHAPTER SEVEN

FATHERING IN LATE ADOLESCENCE (AGES 15–18)

For most teenagers, late adolescence coincides with the entry into high school. This change creates a challenging adjustment for most young people, a mixture of intimidation and excitement. The high school experience is bounded by anxiety at both the entry and departure points. Starting and graduating high school can both feel scary.

Reviewing research on the transition to high school, Mizelle (see ERIC DIGEST, EDO-PS–99–11, August 1999) has this to say: "The importance of parents being involved in their young adolescent student's transition from middle school to high school can hardly be overestimated. . . .When parents are involved in their child's high school experiences, students have higher achievement. . .are better adjusted. . .and are less likely to drop out of school." So to be a connected father at this stage, stay involved in your teenager's schooling.

The impact of this transition on mid-adolescents is usually enough to break them out of their short-term preoccupation with what's happening presently because evidence of an exciting future is all around them and too enticing to ignore. They see and hear what older students are doing, and, awed and inspired, late adolescents start looking ahead and looking forward to more worldly experience. People not much older than themselves are acting in grown-up ways, doing things like getting licensed to drive a car, holding part-time jobs, enjoying later curfews, going on dates, going to parties, and even having significant romances.

With so much older age activity now within tempting reach, attending to responsibilities at home and at school can be harder to do. For this reason, it helps if a father can take the lead as a connection maker, keeping his late adolescent well "tied in" to positive social relationships that support constructive challenge. At school, he can insist that his high school freshman join an established organization like band or theatre or a sports team that provides both social membership and a regular schedule of demands to meet. Outside of school he can support enrolling in a youth group at church, regularly seeing extended family, or being part of some volunteer service effort, all of which provide direction, identity, and affiliation to encourage responsible growth. As a father, you must set a "growing up" agenda that is strong enough to compete with the one your teenager is now creating on his own.

Come this age, many teenagers develop an informal "to do" list of new activities they want to experience that constitute a rite of passage, activities that will officially accredit (to self and peers, if not to parents) how the young person is growing up. In pursuit of this agenda, high school increases the late adolescent desire to act older.

Fathers find themselves in a peculiar position during this time. They would also like to see older behavior (having their own "to do" list in mind for the teenager), but the two lists can be as different as what each means by the phrase "to act grown up.'" The father's list describes more grown-up responsibilities. His teenager's list describes more grown-up adventures.

The Father's "to do" list might include:	The Late Adolescent's "to do" list might include:
Get part-time job,	Go driving with older students,
Give more household help,	Go to a college party,

Earn and save money,	Skip school with friends,
Pay more of own expenses,	Pass for adult and get served alcohol,
Independently do schoolwork,	Party at home when parents are away,
Plan for after high school.	Have some sexual experience.

Something about the two lists doesn't quite jibe. The father's requires more self-discipline; the teenager's list entails more self-indulgence. So what is a father to do? He needs to push *two* agendas.

First, he needs to use the high school years to help his teenager gather as much power of responsibility as possible so that, come graduation, the young person is prepared to make the smoothest transition into successfully managing a more independent life. And second, the father needs to use the high school years to encourage his teenager to gather as much power of maturity as possible. Come graduation, he wants that young person to be sufficiently seasoned by experience to be able to act with maximum personal effectiveness when confronted with the normal frustrations and unexpected problems that are part of daily life. Fulfilling these roles, as responsibility planner and maturity builder, a father can make a major parenting contribution in late adolescence.

ENCOURAGING MORE RESPONSIBILITY

Late adolescence ends in anxiety: stepping off into more independence than one has known before, knowing one is not fully prepared for all the new freedom and responsibility ahead. It's scary, and that's okay. It is less scary, however, if a father, starting freshman year, has taken the lead in talking with his teenager about independence requirements.

For example, here is how one father started responsibility planning freshman year. "I did it with each of my kids. At the beginning of freshman year in high school, we sat down to discuss graduation requirements. 'Graduation requirements?' they would ask. 'I'm not going to graduate for four years. I don't need to think about that. That's what school counselors are for, not you.' And I'd agree. 'I'm not talking academic requirements, I'm talking about independence requirements—what knowledge and skills you're going to need to responsibly take care of yourself out in the world after you graduate. The time to start laying out that schedule of preparation is now.' And then I give them a focal question to be answered year by year, and together we start filling the answers in. Freshman year: *What daily support are we providing for you that you could learn to do for yourself?* Maybe waking yourself up in the morning for school, doing your own laundry, shopping and cooking one night a week for family, as we transfer those and other service responsibilities over to you. Sophomore year: *What basic expenses that we've paid for could we give you monthly money to cover and learn to budget for yourself?* Maybe lunch money, recreation spending, clothing costs, as we transfer those money management responsibilities to you. Junior year: *What employment can you find to earn money for what we would normally not provide and start paying some of your own expenses?* Maybe for a trip, a car, or membership in a gym, as we transfer some of that earning and saving responsibility to you. Senior year: *What approximation of full freedom can you manage that we controlled for you before?* Maybe control over social schedule and going out, schoolwork, time for rest, and meeting family obligations, as we transfer more of that self-regulation responsibility to you."

What the father in this case wanted was to have his son graduate with enough well-earned confidence to be able to declare: "Because I've learned how to take care of myself, I feel ready for more independence now." In this case the dad focused on four major categories of responsibility: overseeing self-maintenance and personal care; mastering basic expenses within a limited budget, employment, and earning and saving money; getting school work done; and managing social freedom.

Think about it. What skills for more independent living do you feel are important to establish prior to your teenager's graduation? Write them down. Then space the acquisition of those skills out over the four high school years and decide when and how they will be taught and encouraged. Without this type of preparation, a young person graduates into the next degree of freedom, say going away to college, without practical self-management tools. Floundering and failing to catch hold of new responsibilities, now she must learn from hard experience skills that a proactive father during late adolescence might have taught.

For some young people, the mid-adolescent preoccupation with "what's happening now" continues into high school and late adolescence, creating a significant distraction from academic focus. The accomplishment of schoolwork, for example, can become an active source of conflict between the teenager, who wants to ignore or put it off, and the parents, who press to get it done. As the performance parent, the father knows that the best preparation for the hard job of managing independence after graduation is working hard in high school now.

Living like there's no time but the present, like there's no tomorrow, your teenager in late adolescence may still cling to a life ruled by immediate gratification. Because you understand that this is not a viable model for getting through high school, much less making one's way in the world, you wait for a chance to make an intervention that can make a difference, the chance to make a *future contact*. In other words, you wait to hear your daughter talk about future dreams, specific interests, or even plans, and then offer to help her contact someone in that field of activity who can provide more information.

When she mentions one day the possibility of attending a certain college or taking up a certain line of work after high school, you make her an immediate offer. "I'll take you to visit that college." "I'll find someone in that line of work you can talk to." In each case, you are looking to create some future contact to provide more perspective in her life. Your daughter may be locked into the present because she cannot see beyond it. Helping her clarify a future goal is one way to break the present's hold. A college or occupational objective can organize and direct her behavior by causing her to connect what she needs to do in school with the future she desires.

So visit the college in which she expressed interest. Get her an appointment with an admissions counselor and then get out of the way so she can hear the academic requirements for getting in. By getting out of the way, you make it clear that this contact is for her, not for you, just like the schoolwork necessary to get her there is now between herself and her future, not between herself and her parents. The same strategy applies when the future contact talks to her about some line of work after high school. The informant tells her what qualifications, training requirements, and application procedures must be met to enter that occupation.

Late adolescence is when some short-term goal setting can begin. The starting question is: "After high school, what?" Helping anchor these early life goals in a concrete reality is part of the father's exit planning role.

ANXIETY AT THE DEPARTURE POINT

Late adolescence is about getting ready for independence. Approaching the age when high school ends and a further step out into the world will be taken, the late adolescent has a mixed response to the next degree of freedom. On one hand, the older teenager is excited by the prospect of living free from parental surveillance and interference, but on the other hand the teenager often feels anxious.

Clearly, the late adolescent is not entirely ready for the separation and responsibility that more independence brings. No matter how thorough your late adolescent preparation is, significant knowledge will be lacking, significant skills will be wanting, significant experience will be missing, and significant discipline will be undeveloped.

Remember that all of this is normal. The best a father, with all his work, can hope for is about 60 percent readiness. The late adolescent has to pick up the balance from experiencing the Big R—Reality. Your teenager has to experience trial and error and recovery as well, and in doing so she will learn to function independently of you. If the late adolescent waits to separate until he or she is entirely ready for independence, separation will never happen. For the young man or young woman, the courage of late adolescence is to leave partly unprepared, and the courage of parents is to let the unprepared young person go. Remember that anxiety at the point of departure is natural for everyone, not just the teenager. The father's job here is to confront fears with faith that both encourages and reassures.

For the late adolescent, fears of challenges ahead often combine with losses that can make leaving harder to bear. What kinds of losses? Consider just a few.

- *Loss of friends:* As old friends scatter to different destinations and begin to follow different paths in life, your teenager will be confronted with having to make a new social circle.
- *Loss of living at home:* As leaving home becomes a reality, your teenager will feel more out of touch with family.

- *Loss of support:* As part of taking on more responsibility for independence, your teenager will be less reliant on your daily parental care.
- *Loss of competence:* As old surroundings are left behind, your teenager will experience a degree of ineffectiveness at first in coping with the demands from living and working in a new locale.
- *Loss of security:* As the familiar, predictable, and comfortable social world of school is ending, your teenager will enter an unfamiliar, unpredictable, and uncomfortable larger world.

No wonder your late adolescent is anxious: It feels like starting over! Since most teenagers have some degree of ambivalence about leaving home at the end of late adolescence, you should be careful to listen for three kinds of statements of fear: *insecurity, inadequacy,* and *doubt.*

- Insecurity: "I don't know if I can live this far away from home!"
- Inadequacy: "I don't know if I can take care of myself by myself!"
- Doubt: "I don't know if I am making the right choice!"

Each statement expresses some worries that need to be taken seriously. Remember that your own anxiety during this transition point is normal, but try to find outlets of expression other than your teenager, because your worries will only exacerbate her own. What your teenager most needs from you are statements of encouragement and support, not expressions of your worry to worsen his own. Most important, be a confidence builder at this juncture, not a confidence breaker. Affirmatively try to answer concerns:

- In response to insecurity at being away from home, say: "You are no further away from us than e-mail and the phone, and we will visit."
- In response to a sense of inadequacy about self-care, say: "You've been taking good care of yourself all senior year."
- In response to doubting the choice of where to go, say: "If this turns out not to be the right decision there will be other choices you can make."

Know that your late adolescent not being entirely ready for more independence is not a problem to be solved, but a reality to accept. Know that by expressing worry you just add to his or her existing anxiety. Know that what is needed from you is the unwavering support of your unshakable faith: "I believe you have what it takes to make this next step."

BUDGET PLANNING

Just because your late adolescent has reached graduation age doesn't mean he or she has necessarily finished high school or is obligated to live away from home. Some young people may go on to further education or training, enjoying some or full financial support. Many others, however, continue to live at home after finishing high school (or not) and face going directly into the world of work, perhaps paying parents rent, perhaps saving money to finance moving out at a later time.

They discover that, although they would like to move out and maybe share an apartment with friends, the entry-level employment they can get doesn't pay enough to cover the expense. So they are stuck, "trapped" at home (at least that's how they feel), yet still grateful that they have a place to stay. This usually makes for an awkward arrangement—dependent on parents, the adolescent is ready to live free of parental restraint when some parental restrictions and demands still apply.

In his exit-planning role, a father who foresees this situation can find it helpful to do some budget planning with his beleaguered teenager who doesn't want to stay, but can't envision an affordable way to go.

"I can't afford to move out," complains the 18-year-old. "Sure you can," gently corrects his father. "It's true you can't afford to move out and have the lifestyle you've grown accustomed to living with us. You're going to have to live on less, without a lot of the comforts of home. Starting out on your own means living on less money, in simpler circumstances, than you do with us, and that's okay. That's how it is for most people. That's just a reality. If you'd like, I can help you figure out what you can afford."

Sitting down with his son, a father does some expense calculation to help the teenager figure out how much income it would take to achieve the short-term goal of moving out on his own. They brainstorm categories of expenses and estimate how much per month more independence would cost. When the sum exceeds what the young man can make working full time at his job, they begin another budget that is based more on necessities than wants, the bare minimum budget. "Most people have to get by on less money than they would like," explains the father. "The secret is finding ways to cut back and live on what you earn." And the son looks at living with no cable television, no Internet, no cell phone, no car, and a host of other comforts he will have to do without. "This will be tough to do," says the son. "But I think you're tough enough to do it," encourages his dad. "I believe you have the maturity it takes."

What strengthens "toughness" at this age is maturity. More than anything else I have seen in counseling, what undercuts and delays maturity is a significant history of adolescent substance use.

HOW SUBSTANCE USE CAN DELAY MATURITY

To grow up, a late adolescent must be encouraged to mature, and a father needs to recognize the kinds of choices that accomplish this goal. One way to appreciate mature choices is to understand what their opposite, immature choices, look like. A teenager who gets into significant substance use offers an instructive example of what happens when mature development is arrested.

Consider an 18-year-old in treatment for substance abuse that began at age 13. "I grew up using a lot of drugs," she declares in a family group session that includes her father. "No you didn't," he disagrees. "No one grows up using a lot of drugs, because heavy drug use keeps people from growing up. Every time the going got tough, you either got drunk or high or wasted."

And the father is correct, because drug abuse commonly interferes with development of a child's maturity by causing her to disengage from normal challenges arising in life that must be met if growing up is to occur.

- How can a child grow up if unhappy feelings, instead of being faced, are continually escaped?
- How can a child grow up if responsibilities, instead of being met, are continually resisted?
- How can a child grow up if honesty about what is happening, instead of being admitted, is continually denied with lies?
- How can a child grow up if work, instead of being accomplished, is continually shunned?
- How can a child grow up if commitments, instead of being honored, are continually broken?
- How can a child grow up if self-discipline, instead of being developed, is continually neglected?
- How can a child grow up if hard decisions, instead of being made, are continually put off?

Life is just a series of challenges that only increase as you grow. Young people learn maturity from directly engaging with the demands these challenges create, gaining skills for effective coping as they grow. Unfortunately, substance abuse tends to lead the young person off the path of engagement, onto the path of avoidance and escape.

Rather than maturing with every new challenge met, he or she remains immature by choosing "the easy way out," selecting strategies and responses for ease of convenience in the moment. In this evasive process, significant opportunity for learning and growth is lost. This is how many young substance abusers actually "outsmart" themselves, winning the battle ("I got away with lying about skipping in high school," she boasts) but losing the war ("I finally dropped out because I got so far behind," she admits).

One bulwark against substance abuse in particular, and protracted immaturity in general, is being encouraged to effectively cope with the challenges of life. This instruction is part of a father's leadership role, should he choose to assume it. For example, because you encourage your daughter to work problems through to a successful conclusion, she arranges for extra math help at school to recover her footing after not understanding quadratic equations. Thanks to your support, she not only increases math knowledge but gains confidence in her capacity to master a difficult challenge.

As the father of a high school student, one of your jobs is to consistently encourage choices that are mature and to identify and discourage those choices that are not. You do this by keeping an eye out for the frustrations and adversities she faces, watching to see if she elects immature or mature responses, of the kinds listed below.

Immature	*Mature*
Acting victim.	Taking charge.
Blaming others.	Accepting responsibility.
Being defensive.	Being receptive.
Acting defeatist.	Acting persistent.
Seeing no choice.	Creating alternatives.
Becoming impulsive.	Becoming disciplined.
Escaping the problem.	Engaging the problem.
Distorting reality.	Keeping perspective.
Acting emotionally.	Acting rationally.
Giving up.	Trying harder.
Refusing advice.	Seeking help.

A father's job is to recognize and encourage mature choice-making in his late adolescent. In many cases, urging mature choices on a teenager who wants a quick or easy way out can be unrewarding work for a father to do. If his daughter is used to taking the easy way out, she may resent and resist his hard advice. Here's an example of what I mean. Your daughter tries out for the cheerleading squad, doesn't make it, and complains: "I'm never going to work that hard for anything again! What's the point?" But you don't want to support this defeatist attitude. You want her to respond with persistence because you know the maturity she learns in high school is what she will carry forward after graduation. So you say something like this: "I understand why you're feeling disappointed, but I hope you either try out again or consider some other organization to join. *If you can't get exactly what you want, then figure out the next best thing and go for that.*" You are encouraging her to make effective and engaging choices and helping her not get stuck in ineffective and disengaging choices. One way you can ratify the power of mature decisions for her is to ask her a simple question: "Which list of choice-making in life would cause you to feel best about yourself?" For most adolescents, there is no contest. The righthand list of mature decisions is self-affirming; the left is self-defeating.

SUPPORTING "THE RULES OF ENGAGEMENT"

Growth is a gathering of power, from dependence in infancy to independence in adulthood. The task of adolescents is to increasingly learn to manage on their own, gathering confidence in their capacity to count on themselves in reliable and constructive ways. *Maturity is the capacity for effective coping,* and it is learned from engaging with challenging demands in life when they arise. Maturity is arrested when those demands are escaped, when young people are indulged and taken care of too much, when they rebel too strongly against their own self interests, or resort to substance use, and when they avoid what feels difficult or unpleasant or painful.

Come the high school years, you need to assess the development of your teenager's level of maturity, because if it is lagging, you still have time with the young person at home to help it grow. From my counseling experience, I have noticed nine areas of decision making that commonly contribute to a young person's maturity, each one supporting a different category of effective choice.

To help assess your teenager's growth, use the following example of two late adolescents. Contrasted across nine categories of engagement, X and Y are both 17 years old, the same sex, from comparable backgrounds, comparable abilities, with comparable life experience except in one respect. From the age of 12, X has been taking the "easy" way of avoidance when confronted with hard situations; while Y has been taught to step up and deal directly with normal hardships along the way. X has more often elected to disengage from the demands of reality; Y has more often elected to engage with those same demands.

X:	Y:	
Breaks promises to self and others,	COMMITMENT	Keeps promises to self and others,
Doesn't finish what is started,	COMPLETION	Finishes what is started,

Doesn't maintain continuity of important effort,	CONSISTENCY	Maintains continuity of important effort,
Avoids dealing with painful situations,	CONFRONTATION	Encounters painful situations,
Lets impulse rule over judgment,	CONTROL	Lets judgment rule over impulse,
Disowns results of actions,	CONSEQUENCES	Owns results of actions,
Decides by default when deciding gets hard,	CLOSURE	Decides by hard choice when deciding gets hard,
Shuts up about or acts out hard feelings,	COMMUNICATION	Speaks up about and talks out hard feelings,
Gives up what has mattered to self and family.	CARING	*Holds onto* what has mattered to self and family.

What is the outcome for X? At the age of 17, he has a lot of catching up to do:

- By repeatedly breaking promises to self, X has *lost* some faith in his *capacity for self-reliance.*
- By repeatedly starting much but finishing little, X has *lost* some confidence in his *capacity to follow through and meet personal goals.*
- By repeatedly being unable to keep up a healthy daily regimen, X has *lost* some *capacity for discipline and self-care.*
- By repeatedly choosing to escape personal pain, X has *lost* some *capacity to tolerate and admit emotional hurt.*
- By repeatedly giving into the lure of immediate gratification, X has *lost* some *capacity to resist temptation.*
- By repeatedly denying the connection between bad choice and bad consequence, X has *lost* some *capacity for personal responsibility.*
- By repeatedly letting circumstances determine difficult decisions, X has *lost* some *capacity for mental toughness.*

- By repeatedly refusing to express hard feelings directly, X has *lost* some *capacity for open and honest communication.*
- By repeatedly betraying what has traditionally mattered, X had *lost* some *capacity to feel positively connected to self and family.*

Understanding these possible costs, you can encourage your teenagers along a path of maturity during their late adolescent years. You can encourage them to make hard choices that will engage with challenge, increase effectiveness, empower independence, and affirm sense of worth. You can communicate these "rules of engagement."

1. "Stick to your promises and agreements."
2. "Finish what you begin."
3. "Keep doing what you know is good for you."
4. "Face hard situations courageously."
5. "Use good judgment to resist bad temptation."
6. "Own your bad decisions so you can learn from your mistakes."
7. "Learn to choose between hard choices, when hard choices are all you have."
8. "When you feel hurt or have problems, talk them out."
9. "Don't betray what you truly care about, or you will betray yourself."

In my experience, a late adolescent who has learned to follow these rules of engagement is less likely in high school, and in the more dangerous stage of adolescence that comes after, to make self-defeating or self-destructive decisions from lack of judgment, peer pressure, impulsivity, or substance abuse.

The job of the father during his teenager's late adolescence is to help him or her gather more knowledge and skills to increase responsibility, and learn to make choices that engage with life challenges to increase maturity.

CHAPTER EIGHT

FATHERING IN TRIAL INDEPENDENCE (AGES 18–23)

If you believe that when your son or daughter graduates from high school you also graduate from active parenting as a father, think again. Typically, adolescence isn't over for another five years, or even longer. As Jeffrey Arnett writes in his book *Emerging Adulthood* (2004), "For today's young people, the road to adulthood is a long one. They leave home at age 18 or 19, but most do not marry, become parents, and find a long-term job until at least their late twenties. From their late teens to their late twenties they explore the possibilities available to them in love and work, and move gradually toward making enduring choices.... To be a young American today is to experience both excitement and uncertainty, wide-open possibility and confusion, new freedoms and new fears."

In many ways, now the most daunting stage of adolescence, the one I call *trial independence,* has begun, and with it the most delicate stage of your fathering.

Now the young person is likely living away from home for the first time (usually with roommates) and working at a job, pursuing further education, or both. Although equipped with more desire for independence, the young person usually does not possess sufficient skills to carry it off entirely without mishap. Trial independence demands more responsibility than most young people can initially handle.

Just think about the seemingly simple challenge of having a roommate—a complex lesson in interdependent living. Now young people have to learn to divide expenses and space, share common resources and obligations, cooperate with each others' needs and schedules, depend on mutual commitments, tolerate personality and lifestyle differences, communicate about disagreements and resolve conflicts, and get along with someone whose habits one does not always like. And all this is only one challenge among many at this age.

There's so much freedom and temptation for a young person to manage. Among your teenager's cohort of friends, few seem to have a clear direction in life, and when it comes to finding a firm footing in independence, many are slipping and sliding and breaking commitments to their detriment. There are broken resolutions and promises, broken romantic relationships, broken loan agreements, broken deadlines, broken job obligations, broken credit arrangements, broken leases, broken educational programs, and even broken laws.

What young people discover, no matter how well prepared they are in late adolescence, is that assuming responsible independence is much more complicated than they thought. In addition, most may have no clear direction in life, no particular path into the future they want to follow.

Peers are a mixed blessing. To the good, the camaraderie and support of friends create a community of care that now compliments family. To the bad, because of the social chaos of "crazy" acting friends at this time, it can be hard to keep one's composure, capacity for judgment, and ability for thoughtful (not impulsive) choice. It can be hard not to lose your head when those around you are losing theirs to anxiety from uncertainty, to alcohol and other substance abuse, to escape into constant partying, to denial that choices today have consequences tomorrow.

Anxieties abound in the face of challenges that often feel overwhelming. And as young people fail to hold up all essential responsibilities and meet all commitments, there is a powerful drop in self-esteem from an agonizing sense of developmental incompetence: "Here I am 21 years old, and I can't get my life together. I keep screwing up and still can't figure out what I want to do with my life!"

LIFESTYLE STRESS

At the same time lifestyle stress comes into play. Many young people at this age do not take good care of themselves as power of want triumphs over power of will, as impulse overrules judgment, and as temptation overcomes restraint. They stress themselves with

- sleep deprivation and chronic fatigue,
- non-nourishing eating habits,
- procrastination over obligations,
- evasion of responsibility,
- failure to meet commitments,
- lies to keep up appearances,
- indebtedness from credit spending,
- nonstop socializing and partying,
- escape into alcohol and other drugs,
- nagging self-criticism for failing to keep life together at such an advanced age.

In consequence, many young people in this last adolescent passage go through periods of despondency, confusion, uncertainty, guilt, shame, anxiety, and exhaustion, seeking short-term relief in substance use that often makes problems worse. From my experience counseling adolescents this age, the three to five years after high school is a period of extremely heavy and varied substance use, interpersonally and personally disorganizing the lives of many young people at this vulnerable stage. Although I have mentioned substance use earlier in this book, now it needs to be discussed again. Thus if your child gets into serious difficulty from repeated acts of poor judgment at this time, ask yourself: "Might substance use have had a role in the unhappy events that occurred? If there had been no drinking or using, would the same choices have been made?"

Many times, no such detective work by a concerned father is required. For example, at 3:00 A.M. a dad is called down to the local jail by his 22-year-old son, who says, "I don't know what happened. The evening started with me just having a good time having a few drinks; next thing I know I'm being taken in for doing stuff I don't exactly remember, stuff I can't believe I did!" Rather than respond to his statement at the moment, the father takes the time to think out what he wants to share with his son. This is what he decides to say.

"Substance use is pretty simple," he explains, "in my day and now in yours. It's always been about getting freedom—*freedom for* feeling good or *freedom from* feeling bad. And it works, but the freedom carries risk because it affects your state of caring and choices that you make. What feels good at the start can turn bad at the end. Like last night, you started out sober and *careful,* then you started drinking and felt *carefree,* and finally you got drunk, *not caring* what you did, and got thrown in jail for doing what you now see wasn't wise or right. You got your freedom, but you lost your judgment." Although it's hard, the father lets his son put in the jail time and pay the legal fees, hoping he will learn to drink in moderation.

Here's one ground rule for a father during trial independence: Do not rescue your son or daughter from the consequences that ignorant, impulsive, intoxicated, or unwise choices may have caused. Remember, now reality has become the most important teacher in your child's life, and your role has become a tutorial one, to help that young person sort out painful lessons to be learned while you are careful to be nonjudgmental, noncritical. You didn't want this to happen to your child, but since it did, you want the maximum educational benefit to occur.

While you believe in the value of informal education from hard experience, this is an adolescent stage when you also have to be watchful of the formal education that you financially support. Consider the all-too-common practice of educational extortion, whereby the young person keeps claiming student status to justify continued dependency on parental resources and thereby exempt themselves from more grown-up responsibility. For example, a young woman who has flunked out of two college programs with failures, incompletes, and drops now asks her father to support a third attempt on the same old terms: "Just pay my tuition and living expenses and I promise to work harder than I did before." Sometimes a father, feeling guilty that he did not maintain a closer bond with his daughter, and faulting himself for her lack of responsibility at this advanced age, will end up enabling the dependent behavior he finds so troubling by bailing her out once again with his financial support. After all, he wants her to get a college degree for the later employment benefit it may confer.

This time, however, the father wants to continue his commitment to her college support, but makes a change in how it will be provided: "Of course I will pay for your college, but from now on I'm going to do it from the back end, not the front. You go to work and earn enough money to pay your tuition at the beginning of each semester, and I will reimburse you for every course you pass and complete. As for your living expenses, I will be paying only some, not all, of those. You'll have to study to be able to go to college, and you'll have to work to support getting through it. I believe that is the most constructive way." Although his daughter may not like the conditions, he takes this stand so she can learn to take responsibility for her further education.

THE PROBLEM OF FRUSTRATION

For a father who is committed, engaged, settled down, and practical, it can be hard to empathize with a "grown child" in her early twenties who is uncommitted, disengaged, unsettled, and unrealistic. It's hard for the man, when her poor choices lead to unhappy outcomes, to remember that this is an extremely vulnerable age—she is old enough to be considered adult but not yet competent enough to entirely act that way.

"I can't understand how someone this old can make choices this stupid!" complains a father in counseling. "It's not like she didn't know better. Besides, I'm tired of her bad choices causing problems in my life." "So," I might ask, "since age 20 you made nonstop good decisions?" "My life doesn't have anything to do with it!" he objects. "It has everything to do with it," I disagree. "People make stupid choices all their lives. If we could lay out your twenty-first year today, we'd see all kinds of decisions—affecting home, college, jobs, relationships, finances, the law, and substances, for example—that you probably wouldn't mind taking back if you could." "Well, maybe so," he grumbles, "but I just want her to get her problems behind her, to get them over." This is a common case of fathering fatigue.

There's nothing wrong in feeling tired from parenting during your child's final stage of growing up, but you need to be realistic, and you definitely need to keep perspective. Realistically, the biggest problems in life are not going to be behind your teenager once adolescence is done. They're going to be ahead of her, in her adult future. These last years of active fathering create the foundation for her relationship with you as an adult. So hanging in there at the end of her adolescence counts for a lot.

Part of a father's job in trial independence is to help hone his child's problem-solving and recovery skills, because she'll depend on this resourcefulness as an adult. So every problem she encounters or creates during this final stage of growing up is an opportunity to grow a little stronger for the years ahead. For the father who feels he's done all he can, or at least wants relief from his child's ongoing hardships and intermittent crises, there are a lot of tempting bailing-out points during a child's trial independence. But he must hang in there—to listen, not to rescue, and to provide mentoring advice if asked, always respecting her right to make her own decisions, because it is her life to manage.

THREE VULNERABILITIES OF TRIAL INDEPENDENCE

Trial independence is about establishing social separation from family and becoming self-governing and more self-supporting. What the late adolescent fears to some degree comes true: The task of successfully assuming independence is too much for most anyone to master right away, so there is a periodic sense of not measuring up to the task.

In trial independence, feelings of inadequacy can seriously undermine self-esteem.

By acting unwisely or suffering a setback, a young person can encourage feelings of inadequacy in three ways: by *self-criticism*, by *worry*, and by *despair*.

- The *self-criticism* can be: "What's the matter with me?"
- The *worry* can be: "What's going to happen to me if I keep going on this way?"
- The *despair* can be: "This just goes to show that I'll never learn!"

Having found herself guilty on one or more of these charges, self-doubts can be worsened if the father directs similar charges at his daughter.

- Feeling frustrated, he may point out her failings with criticism: "What's the matter with you?"
- Feeling scared, he may predict worse to come with worry: "What's going to happen to you if you keep going on this way?"
- Feeling discouraged, he may echo her despair: "This just goes to show that you'll never learn!"

If there is one golden rule for you to follow during this bumpy passage through trial independence, it is this: *Refrain from expressions of criticism, worry, and despair,* because your son or daughter is prone to those responses already. Rather than making your child's vulnerability worse, you are better served, and so is your son or daughter, by providing emotional support.

- Instead of criticism, give an expression of *encouragement:* "Just because you didn't do it right the first time doesn't mean you can't get it right the next."
- Instead of worry, give a vote of *confidence:* "This experience will only make you wiser in the years ahead."
- Instead of despair, give a statement of *faith:* "I believe you have what it takes to find your footing and your way."

TRANSITIONING FROM MANAGER TO MENTOR

It may be difficult not to express criticism, frustration, disappointment, anger, even despair, but such responses will only deepen an existing wound, and may discourage the young person from seeking what she really needs in her father—mentoring based on your life experience. Both of you are better served if you express confidence in her capacity to learn from mistakes, and she uses that confidence to support her will to keep trying.

At this last stage of your child's adolescence, you must change your role from being *manager* (providing supervision and regulation) to becoming *mentor* (providing consultation and advice—when asked). If you barge in and try to direct or control her troubled life at this late stage (when a job has been lost and bills are past due), you run two risks. Either you will rescue her from learning life lessons taught by accepting responsibility or you will reduce communication with a daughter who refuses to be managed anymore.

As mentor, however, you can respect her right to make her own decisions, to benefit from the good and recover from the bad. And you can offer the benefit of your experience and ideas if they can be of service as your last-stage adolescent tries to figure out how to choose her way out of the difficulty she has chosen her way into. To effectively discharge this new parenting role as mentor, however, you must let go of all corrective discipline. You are no longer in the business of structuring your daughter's life, overseeing her conduct, setting limits to her freedom, or applying consequences to discourage repetition of mistakes or misdeeds. It is not your job to decide what is best for her or to bend her life to your beliefs. Facing real world consequences will provide self-discipline enough.

To be an effective mentor means you must be emotionally approachable.

- Express faith, not doubt ("You can do it");
- Be patient, not angry ("Keep after it");
- Provide consultation, not criticism ("You might try this");
- Be understanding, not disappointed ("It's hard to manage independence");
- Demonstrate confidence, not worry ("You have what it takes!").

Many adolescents in this last stage before adulthood lose their independent footing and must be encouraged to learn from sad experience what they did not grasp before: that learning the hard way by profiting from mistakes and taking responsibility for recovery is the only route to maturity. Even mature adolescents usually have some trouble along the way. Your job, through mentoring, is to support the will to keep trying and to be accessible so the young person can call upon your experience, understanding, and advice.

What about the young person who really loses his footing in life and wants to come home to recover? That's fine, and in fact is very common. Adult children returning to live at home have been dubbed in the popular media as "boomerang kids," and they contribute to an increasingly common family change. How common? According to an analysis of recent U.S. Census data (see Nancy Mullens, *USA Today*/Education, March 16, 2006), there were "Fewer empty nests" in 2004 than in 1970. For example, in 1970, 5.64 million males ages 18–24 lived in the parental home compared to 8.01 million in 2004. For females in the same age group, 4.94 million lived at home in 1970 and 6.33 million in 2004.

Should this return home occur, do not rescue your son from unmet obligations. Simply provide a mutually agreed upon time-limited period at home for the young man to regroup—to rethink, to re-solve, and then to reenter the world and struggle with the challenge of trying to claim independence again.

Losing a job, flunking out of college, ending a love relationship, abusing substances, and experiencing financial problems are the five major causes for a young person to return home that I encounter in counseling. For example, consider the case of the son who accepts multiple credit card offers, running up more debt than he can pay. Now he has collection agencies calling and sending letters, and is finding how costly unpaid balances can be. "If you'll just pay off what I owe, I won't let it happen again!" pleads the young man to his father, who offers to help, but not to get him off the hook. "I'll help you after you help yourself first. You earn the money to pay back half of what you owe, and when you do, I'll loan you the other half, to be paid back to me on a schedule you agree to meet. You ran it up; you need to pay it down. I'd be doing you no favor bailing you out of debt that you created. Just so you know, it took me some time to learn how to manage plastic too. Money is always easier to borrow than it is to pay back. If you'd like, I'll work with you on developing a debt recovery plan."

It is important to make clear to your adolescent that coming back home to live for a while is not a right to be assumed. It is a privilege to be earned by maintaining a presence that is consistent with orderly ways parents want to live. There is always the tendency for the grown child to regress to old habits when coming back to stay, and it is reasonable for a father to expect that effort will be made to respect parental needs. So specify what kinds of cooperation you expect from him, and what specific kinds of support you are willing to offer. From what I have seen, these returns work best when parents and a young person clearly understand and agree on how this period of living together will operate.

If your last-stage adolescent cannot maintain this agreement, and some cannot, resenting and resisting and resurrecting old household conflicts about picking up and cleaning up, getting back into heavy-duty parenting is not the answer. Some departures into the reality of true independence are more difficult than are others. If you are a father of a last-stage adolescent who is leaving home in anger because she is neither ready to follow household rules nor feels entirely ready to do without parental support, it's best to accept your daughter's hard emotional place. It is best to give her your blessing of love and good faith. Do what you can to make this an amicable parting by declaring: "I respect that you cannot fit in and follow how we like to live, but I also respect our right to live on terms that work for us. So within the next month you need to make other living arrangements for yourself. Of course, we wish you well on your way and want to see you as always." Leaving under these circumstances must not carry any onus of parental rejection or personal failure.

PUTTING FAILURE IN PERSPECTIVE

Because there seem to be limitless possibilities for failed efforts in trial independence, a father needs to do what he can to turn them to good educational account. For example, spring semester freshman year, a boy awkwardly confesses to his father that he flunked most of his fall courses and was placed on academic probation.

"I didn't learn anything!" the young man despairingly concludes. About to angrily agree with his son, the father catches himself, pauses to cool down and think, and then thinks to say, "Tell me how you spent your time." That's when his son's list of non-academic activities pours out. "I played online games. I partied late and had a hard time waking up so a lot of times I stayed in bed and skipped a lot of classes. I didn't do much homework or study for tests. I bought a bunch of books, but didn't read them. Most of my time I just hung out with friends, drinking some, and smoking dope."

Now the dad proceeds carefully. "That sounds like a good education to me," he responds. "Nothing good about it," argues his son. "I didn't learn a thing!" "Sure you did," his father disagrees, and then continues: "Play online, party late, don't get enough sleep, don't wake up in the morning, skip classes, don't study for tests, don't read assignments, drink and smoke dope. You learned a lot about how *not* to do college. If you plan to go back next fall, now you know a bunch of activities to stay away from. Of course, you'd have to work this summer and pay us back for classes you flunked because of absences before we'll pay for you next fall."

Failure? As the performance parent, you may want to explain that there are only two real failures in life. There is the failure to keep trying because you feel discouraged or fear more failure. And there is the failure to learn from mistakes because you'd rather just forget about them and move on.

There's some tough-love education a father can encourage in his last-stage adolescents who are about to step off into young adulthood, and it has to do with respecting how life experience most often helps a person grow. The message is this: Failure teaches more than success, adversity teaches more than good fortune, hardship teaches more than comfort, and criticism teaches more than compliments. And while you wish success, good fortune, comfort, and compliments, and hope your young adults can enjoy them, you also hope they can be open, honest, determined, and courageous enough to profit from failure, adversity, hardship, and criticism. And you definitely want them to develop discipline for self-sufficiency. That's why, should they go to college, you want to help create the need for them to find some part-time work to do.

A free ride through college can be a problem. "It's like four more years of high school with a lot more room to play" was how one freshman described being subsidized to live away from home. "All bills paid and no parents to check up on you, you can't beat that!" No wonder so many first-year students crash and burn.

Aware of this vulnerability, a father can reduce the risk of failure by increasing some necessity for "self-support," and by this I mean at most providing money to cover basics only—room, board, tuition, fees, that's all. Any money for additional expenses is up to the student to earn. In the words of one father to his son: "Now you've reached the time of life when you must start paying part of your own way."

Lots of students grow older in college without doing much growing up at all when their lifestyle needs are entirely taken care of by parents. For these students, college just protracts dependency and defers demands of adult responsibility. Securing part-time employment while at college has a long list of benefits, a few of which are itemized below.

- Self-respect comes from assuming responsibility for some self-support.
- Being paid for one's labor affirms self-worth.
- A job anchors one in the real working world.
- A job schedule helps organize and schedule the rest of college life.
- Earning an entry-level wage is a reminder of how a college education creates the possibility for earning more.
- Holding a job teaches how to show up on time, to deliver a service, to get along with coworkers, to do as directed, and to meet an organizational need.

In trial independence, to entirely rely on parental support is detrimental to increasing self-sufficiency. By creating the necessity for part-time employment to pay some share of living expenses while in college, a father can encourage this independent growth.

SIGNS THAT TRIAL INDEPENDENCE IS OVER

At this last stage of adolescent growth, fathers can be wearing down. Many begin to wonder: "Does trial independence ever end?" Of course it does. Here are some behaviors that indicate the tasks of adolescence have finally been accomplished and now your son or daughter is ready to enter young adulthood and move on. Check the ones you observe in your child to get a rough fix on where they are in their growth.

Your son or daughter:

- Is bored with partying and does it less.
- No longer keeps a constant late-night schedule.
- Is less socially preoccupied with the old gang of friends.
- Complains of time passing them by.
- Is fully financially self-supporting.
- Takes responsibility for actions and doesn't blame others.
- Recovers from bad choices and doesn't seek rescue.
- Manages finances without emergency loans from parents.
- Consistently pays own bills.
- Lives within current income.
- Sets work goals for making more money.
- Tires of dead-end jobs.
- Begins planning for the longer-term future.
- Sets sights on job or career path.
- Maintains separate living space.
- No longer stores old belongings with parents.
- Respects parental needs when visiting home.
- Wants to be of adult service and advice to parents.
- Now talks about health insurance and job benefits.
- Socializes with friends who are more settled down.
- Becomes involved or interested in a serious partner relationship.
- Gets married or becomes relationally committed.
- Starts a family.
- Moves away from hometown to pursue a life opportunity.

As a father, it helps to keep these changes in mind so you can recognize the signs of moving on for yourself and for your late adolescent. Seeing them gives you cause for hope, and expressing appreciation of them affirms the progress your son or daughter makes. Often as they enter young adulthood, the young person that seemed an unending source of trouble in trial independence becomes the son or daughter that you now start to miss.

THE FINAL RECKONING

The last task in your fathering through adolescence is one that may be done directly or indirectly. In either case, your son or daughter needs to evaluate the kind of fathering you gave and the influence you've had upon his or her growth. And then, if she so desires, she needs to communicate that evaluation to you. Your job, should this request occur, is to do nothing but give an unconditional hearing. You empathetically listen. You do not defend, correct, or otherwise disagree. On this occasion, you accept her grievances as she sees and feels them so that, with your understanding and acceptance, she can begin to let them go. Now she can proceed to claim and value all the good you gave.

If you ever had the desire to be above reproach or perfect as a father, this is the time to set such vanity aside. Like any father, the best you had to give was that all-too-human mix of strength and weakness, of wisdom and stupidity, of consideration and selfishness, of sensitivity and insensitivity that every parent, in some form or fashion, ends up providing. What you need to understand is that before your young adult can appreciate and embrace the positive about your contribution as a father and freely establish an ongoing relationship of value with you, the negative must be acknowledged, because some hard feelings always stand in the way.

In my counseling, I have come to call the young adult's need for a parental evaluation a "reckoning."' It is your grown child's analysis and summation of your formative role in his or her history. Entering young adulthood, she has started taking a look at herself as an adult. To this end, she begins taking inventory of who she is and how she grew to be that way. Looking back at major influences that shaped her growth, she locates her parents, both of whom made decisions that affected how she turned out. What she realizes is that she grew up partly *because of* and partly *in spite of* who and how they were, her task to recover from the bad and to build on the good. There are always grievances to be acknowledged, each parent's influence evaluated, each parent in for some measure of blame:

- "I felt you favored my brother over me."
- "I felt I could never satisfy you no matter how I tried."
- "When you divorced, I felt I lost my father, and when you re-married I felt I lost you even more."

How you were as a father leaves her with some issues to resolve as an adult.

- "Because of your temper, I'm afraid of anger in my relationships."
- "Because of your temper, I learned to be explosive with my anger, too."
- "Because I never felt I earned or deserved your approval, I go overboard trying to please the one I love."

It's not that you *want* to commit errors or possess the frailties you do. Your human limitations make you a person and a parent who she sometimes found hard to bear and sometimes found wanting. Either way, you left some painful marks on her growth.

In most cases, this evaluation goes sight unseen and sound unheard by fathers because grown children work it out within themselves, with friends, or sometimes with a counselor.

Although most reckonings are not shared directly with a father, when they are they can bring healing. The young person feels her experience is acknowledged, and the father feels humanized in the child's eyes. You can encourage this encounter by inviting it out, saying something like this: "If you ever feel like telling me what it was like having me as a father growing up, the bad and the good, I would like to hear what you have to say. In doing so, I will listen without objection or interruption, just honoring the feelings you have to share, and answering any questions you may have as honestly as I can. I know I was imperfect and you paid a price for things I did you wish I didn't, for things I didn't do you wished I had, and for not measuring up to all you wanted in a dad. So if you ever want to share any of this with me, please know I stand ready to listen."

What the reckoning enables is reconciliation, establishing a working basis for the relationship between father and grown child in the years ahead. The stages of this reconciliation unfold like this.

1. Adult children reconcile the father they wanted with the father they didn't get, the father they didn't want with the father they got.
2. Adult children accept the human being their father turned out to be, and the father accepts and admits that he was in some ways a source of dissatisfaction and pain to his children.
3. Adult children reconcile with themselves by accepting responsibility *not* for how their father did or did not treat them, but for beliefs and behaviors they chose to adapt in response.
4. Adult children acknowledge the negative in their father so they can gratefully reach beyond that hurt and claim the inheritance of positive influences and outcomes he had to give.

As mentioned earlier, in most cases, the adult child reckoning occurs without direct confrontation with the father. Instead, the young person living apart from family creates social and emotional distance as well, often reducing, even cutting off, communication for a while to do the hard work of reconciliation, privately wading through unhappy feelings to reach the positives on the other side.

For a father who felt close to his child, this can be a lonely, scary time, unless he sees the separation for what it is. Then he can resolve to let her know he is lovingly ready to re-engage with his grown child when she is able to find her loving way back to him, when she feels ready to return.

A father at a workshop of mine many years ago explained it this way: "One rose at a time," he called it.

"She was about 23, our daughter, when without explanation, she cut off all communication with us. Stopped coming to see us. Rarely answered our phone calls, and when she did abruptly told us that she'd call us when she felt like talking, and to please not call her. At first we felt really hurt, then really angry. What had we done to deserve such treatment? Then my wife said something really important: 'Suppose this isn't something painful she's doing *against* us; suppose it's something painful she needs to be doing *for* her.' So that's what we decided it was. And to let her know we loved her and were thinking about her, every week I sent her a single red rose with a card that read: 'We love you.' And I did this for about seven months until one day she called, said she wanted to come over and see us, and she did, and we've been lovingly back together ever since. Of course I asked her about the roses, curious to know what she did with them. 'At first,' she said, 'I threw them away. Then I gave them away to friends. And finally I started keeping them, signs that you were keeping me in your heart, one rose at a time.'"

So, should a time for reckoning arrive and distance come between you and your young adult child, have faith, be patient, keep communicating your love, and be ready to resume the relationship after the need for parent evaluation has been satisfied.

A father's job in trial independence is to respect the young person's capacity for responsible choice—not rescue him or her from negative consequences—expressing faith and encouragement to keep trying, encouraging self-sufficiency, and providing mentoring advice upon request.

CHAPTER NINE

MAINTAINING AUTHORITY

Many years ago, in some former "traditional" family time, a mother might have invoked the father's authority by threatening unruly adolescents like this:

"Wait until I tell your father!"
"Wait until your father gets home!"
"We'll see what your father has to say about this!"

The mother's hope was that having to deal with the more distant and stern male parent would be sufficiently dreaded to discourage any more non-compliance, because a major part of the father's role was to keep the children in line when the mother couldn't. He was the big gun of authority.

This extreme division of authority seems not so common today. One survey of high school adolescents, however, found the "father was perceived to be the family authority about three times more often than the mother, although sons tended to see father as boss more often than daughters, who tended to see mother as boss more often than did sons." (See Harris and Howard in *Journal of Youth & Adolescence*, vol.

10, no. 4, 1981.) So fathers may want to be sensitive to how their authority can be perceived more powerfully by teenage children when compared with that of their wives, more often by sons than by daughters. In addition, if the man is a new single-parent father, he needs to appreciate how establishing authority is essential to secure his children. As stated by Carter and McGoldrick in *The Expanded Family Life Cycle* (2005): "Forming a new family requires that the single parent gain credibility and assume power as the sole executor of a family system that once was ruled by two."

RESTRICTIVE AND CONTRIBUTIVE AUTHORITY

The traditional model of paternal authority that has receded with changing times was primarily a restrictive one, based on the power to:

- *prescribe:* make the rules,
- *pursue:* get children to follow the rules,
- *punish:* provide consequences when they do not.

Today, most fathers would not want to limit their authority to such narrow definitions because it inhibits the connection they want to make with children, particularly with adolescents, who may dismiss such fathering as "a power trip."

Actually, fully defined, a father's authority has at least as many positive as negative characteristics. True, there is *restrictive authority* of the structure-giving, supervisory, and corrective kinds (making rules, pursuing compliance, and applying consequences for infractions). However, there are also many functions of *contributive authority* for him to exercise as well. Contributive authority means using the resources and influence at your disposal to act as beneficiary to your children in ways that they appreciate. Here are some common examples:

- *Knowledge giver:* being a source of valuable information and understanding. "If you like, I'll explain it to you."
- *Help giver:* providing assistance in accomplishing a task or solving a problem. "I won't do it for you, but I will give you a hand on that project if you want."

- *Resource giver:* dispensing benefits and providing support. "Suppose I add to what you've earned to help you get what you've been working for?"
- *Permission giver:* allowing freedom that is desired. "Agree to check in, get back on time, and you can go."
- *Leadership giver:* opening up positive possibilities for growth and development. "If you'd like to give that kind of experience a try, I'll set it up for you."
- *Advocacy giver:* standing up on the child's behalf. "I'd like to be at the hearing to make sure your rights are respected."
- *Approval giver:* positively evaluating effort made or outcome achieved. "Congratulations: It took a lot of hard work to make the cut!"

Come adolescence, taking more frequent stands against what his teenagers want, for the sake of their best interests, makes the father increasingly unpopular. The secret for managing your authority during these challenging years is to keep exercising contributive authority while discharging restrictive authority—setting, supervising, and enforcing rules to keep a safe and constructive family structure around your teenage son or daughter. *The more your contributive authority is apparent, the more easily your restrictive authority will be accepted.*

Here's an example. A discouraged father, who can't get his 13-year-old son's cooperation without getting an argument first, is about to cancel their weekend fishing trip together as a consequence for continually challenging his authority. In counseling, he says to me: "I'm tired of having everything I ask for disagreed with, questioned, or delayed! Why should I take my son off to have a good time when he gives me such a hard time?"

The answer I give him is this: "When you feel constantly challenged around your authority, you must find ways to increase positive experiences or you and your son will be left with nothing but negativity. To let your frustration and anger do your thinking for you is counterproductive. Canceling a good time to stop a bad time is tantamount to saying: 'I'm going to keep punishing you until your response to my authority improves!'" Good luck. With this statement, the father has fallen into the adolescent trap, returning negative for negative, ignoring and withholding the positive, forgetting the most fundamental law for creating a viable relationship with his teenager: *no positive deposit, no positive return.*

Taking away a gift of contributive authority (in this case a trip, as resource giver) as a form of restrictive authority (in this case canceling the trip, as punishment giver) is usually self-defeating. The father only ends up giving all of his authority a bad name. Better to keep the two authority functions separate if he can. Think of it this way. Restrictive authority is for instruction and correction; contributive authority is for investment and enhancement. As a father, you want your authority to proceed on the two separate tracks independent of each other, as you keep instructing and correcting where necessary, and as you keep investing and enhancing to nourish the positive all the time. Remember that the teenager complies with your directives for the sake of the good in your relationship, and not out of fear. Two common failings that reduce cooperation with a father's authority are his criticism, which increases unwillingness to cooperate and comply, and his inconsistency, which invites resistance to see if what is said is really meant.

One way to increase the contributive side of the father's authority and the compliant side of the teenagers' behavior, is to create family getaways, times when normal pressures are suspended and problems set aside. They can be as large as a family vacation or as small as going out to eat. In either case, they create a break during which everyone can set tensions aside, enjoy being with each other, feel connected as a family, and be reminded how important those connections really are. A getaway doesn't make problems go away, but the good time created takes the stress off a hard time and helps reenergize a willingness to work things out.

ADOLESCENCE AND PARENTAL AUTHORITY

Think of your authority this way: Every family system is a value system reflecting the beliefs of the parents, no two families subscribing to exactly the same set of guiding beliefs. It is the responsibility of parents to use their authority to set family norms, establish routines, encourage habits, model conduct, monitor behavior, and make rules to teach children healthy values.

Essentially, parental authority is based on four parental rights that children don't think to question, but teenagers do. A father's authority becomes harder for him to assert as it becomes harder for his teenagers to accept. What he considers a proper level of authority, his teenagers increasingly interpret as an inappropriate exercise of power. There are four parental rights the father can exert:

- *Judgment:* the right to evaluate;
- *Knowledge:* the right to know;
- *Determination:* the right to direct;
- *Punishment:* the right to apply sanctions.

The degree of parental authority can be a tricky business. The more children comply with parental authority, the more dependent they are on that authority to direct their behavior and limit their freedom of action. Extremely authoritarian parents often raise extremely dependent children who aren't very experienced with self-direction. A domineering and strict father who prides himself on having children who never dare to step out of line risks sending young people out into the world who, at an advanced age, have to start learning to think and take responsibility for themselves. Extremely permissive parents often raise extremely independent children who act as their own authority from a very early age. Thus the laissez-faire father, who prides himself on letting his children follow their own inclinations, risks sending young people out in the world who, at an advanced age, have to learn how to comply, conform, and cooperate with social authority.

As in most areas of human conduct, when it comes to defining his authority, the father is best served by avoiding extremes. The trick is to find some middle ground that provides a firm and clear structure of rules and restraints but also allows enough latitude of individual choice for adolescents to learn self-governing responsibility. However, if you are going to err in one extreme direction or the other, *it is better for your authority to be too strict than too lax.* Why?

- Because strictness gives structural guidelines for the teenager to live by, and boundaries to live within.

- Because strictness relieves the teenager of responsibility for full freedom of choice.
- Because strictness shows parental caring and willingness to brave unpopularity.
- Because strictness provides protection the teenager can grudgingly consent to.
- Because strictness provides grounds for arguments and resistance, creating the conflict that necessitates communication.

Excessively lax authority provides none of the above.

CONTROL-BASED AND CONCERN-BASED AUTHORITY

Because of the performance pressure he feels to be an effective authority, and perhaps because of a little personal pride mixed in, a father may hold on to the controlled-based authority that he established when his teenager was a little child. Back then, the man's responsibility was to command obedience to keep his son or daughter protected from impulse, temptation, household hazards, and external dangers, and to teach rudimentary rules of personal and social responsibility.

In adolescence, when your authority becomes more frequently contested by the teenager's push for independence, you are usually better served to shift to a more concern-based authority where disagreements do not automatically lead to conflicts over who prevails, who backs down, and what must be worked out. Instead, you take the time to reach beyond and beneath the momentary disagreement between you and your teenager, focusing on your son or daughter's well-being, and in doing so creating a concern-based connection that often makes addressing the difference easier to do. In other words, *before conflict, express concern.*

Instead of walking in from work and getting into a tempting conflict with your daughter for not having done promised yard clean-up, stop to consider what matters more and must come first. Rather than immediately trying to get your way, connect with your daughter: "Before we get into our nightly disagreement, tell me about your day. Did anything happen in your world that we should be talking about first, that I should know?" The father here is not backing off pursuing his daughter about a household responsibility, but he is letting her know that concern for her comes before "controlling" what she does, and he is making a concern-based connection. *When expression of concern precedes effort to control, consent is more likely to be given.*

ADOLESCENT INDEPENDENCE AND ADULT AUTHORITY

Unless dealing with a strong-willed child who has been extremely determined from a very young age (and will only become more so during the teenage years; see Pickhardt, *The Strong-Willed Child,* 2005), the hard push to be more independent of parental authority usually begins in adolescence. As discussed, now teenagers start to question and contest parental rules and requests, push to act on their own terms, and live according to their own beliefs.

At this juncture, it's important for a father to remember that when a teenager argues with his authority it is *not* a sign of disrespect. Ignoring, discounting, and disregarding his authority is disrespect. When protests at unfairness of a father's rule, or arguments to change it, are followed by grudging obedience to that rule, then his authority is still respected. *The criterion for respect is consent, however unhappily given.* Hence the adolescent compromise: The teenager gets to state his objections and have his say, and then the father, sticking to his position, gets to have his way.

Sometimes a father, by playing authority with a little grace and humor, can lighten up the role enough for his teenager to laugh at the contest being played between them. For instance, consider the common adolescent game of "who waits for who?" In this case, a 16-year-old puts off his dad by saying: "I'll do my chores when I get back, after I borrow the car." To which the father replies: "That's fine. If you don't mind waiting for me to give you the car keys so you can go, I don't mind waiting for the chores to be done."

The ultimate goal is to give up parental authority in general, and a father's authority in particular, as older adolescents become more responsibly self-governing. The father gradually lets go of some areas of decision making as his teenager takes them on. So when a father says, "My job is to discipline you until you learn to discipline yourself," the man is explaining that his authority is preparatory, not permanent.

For example, around the last year of high school, supervision and management of homework is often turned over to the young person; the father no longer checks to see what it is and if it is done, no longer gives his son the support of authority. "You must learn to be in charge of your schoolwork now because, when you go to college, I won't be around to help you keep track and keep up with it. I'm bowing out so you can take over. From now on, when it comes to how you perform at school, you have only to answer to you. School is no longer an issue between you and us; it is an issue between you and your future. Better you should struggle to become your own authority and take care of your own education while you are still with us, than do so for the first time when you are away and on your own."

THE PROBLEM OF CONTROL

"What's hardest for me about my kids' adolescence," confessed a father who successfully runs his own small business, "is feeling so helpless so much of the time. All this responsibility as a parent, and so little real control to back it up! As I was told in anger the other day by my 16-year-old: 'Dad, you can't make me and you can't stop me, so get used to it! I'll get home when I want, not when you want! It's up to me!' I wish she wasn't telling me the truth, but she was. Although, she came back earlier from the party than her friends, just like I asked."

By not allowing her declaration of independence to back him off or back him out of his daughter's life, the father provides safe and healthy guidelines for her to live by. What he controls are the limits on her freedom and expectations for responsibility that he sets. What she controls is her willingness to go along with his requests, which in this case (having saved face with her objections) she chose to do.

Come adolescence, teenagers let dads know that the conduct of cooperation has changed. You can still get them to comply, but you're going to face more resistance—more argument and delay. This is when it becomes clear that you never did have control over your children, even when they were very small. Even back then they were governed by their own choices, not yours. It was just easier to get them to agree when they were smaller.

For some fathers, adolescence can be a frustrating experience if their sense of effectiveness is closely tied to being in control. Now you are forced to confront a humbling reality: Your authority depends on their consent—their willingness to go along with what you want. Instead of power of control, what you really have are ways to influence their consent, discipline strategies to use when it comes to encouraging them to do what you want and to stop doing what you don't want. *A father cannot control the teenager's choices about how to act; he can control his own.* For authoritarian fathers, this can be a hard reality to accept.

"I can't control my teenager!" "I can't make my teenager do what I want!" complains a father who ascribes more power to his authority than it can actually possess. "I've tried everything!" he laments, but in reality he has only run out of the will to keep trying. "I keep striking out!" In counseling, because he's just given me a performance metaphor he believes in, I ask: "What percent of the time do you expect yourself to prevail?" "All the time," he immediately responds. "Bat 1.000, is that what you're telling me?" I reply. "You know better than that. In the great baseball game of life, if we're really good, if we really get on a hot streak, .300 plus is about the best we can do. Why should you do any better in parenting than at the plate? You're confusing effort with outcome. One hundred percent effort, you can strive for that. But not one hundred percent outcome, because that you don't control. When it comes to conflicts with your teenager, you're going to win some, lose some, and compromise more than you ever thought you would. That's just how it is. And you'll get booed more often than you're cheered. But remember this, your teenager isn't going to bat any better than you."

A father's authority earns him more conflict and disapproval with his teenagers during adolescence. He can no longer be just a friend to them, as he mostly was in their childhood—fun buddy and best companion. Now there will be more times when his parental responsibility dictates that he must sacrifice that friendship on the alter of authority, sometimes taking stands for his teenagers' best interests, against what they want, earning unpopularity, not gratitude, in response. Get used to it: *During adolescence, your teenagers will often find your invasive, restraining, and directing force as their father an intrusive, offensive, and unwarranted denial of the privacy, freedom, and independence that they now fervently desire.* The friend you were now sometimes becomes an adversary in their eyes. Thankless parenting has arrived. It's time to get your parental discipline together, using instruction and correction to influence your teenager to act "according to family values and within family rules." (See Pickhardt, *Positive Discipline,* 2004.) You use discipline to help get your teenager to do what you want and to stop doing what you don't want.

DISCIPLINE STRATEGIES

What are some discipline strategies through which a father asserts authority? Consider five, each one connecting father to adolescent, each one showing how a father intends to be counted on and involved in the conduct of the young person's life, often in ways his teenager may not like.

1. *Explanation* is the power to persuade. "Here is what I need to have you do and this is why." Rules without reasons are often resisted by willful children and rebellious adolescents who bridle against that parental statement of arbitrary authority, "Because I said so, that's why!" Explanation can provide justification for cooperation. Rules with reasons can convince: "Okay, I see why that's important."

Of course, explanation can also invite arguments from adolescents who like to disagree. However, even in this case, explanation can serve a father well because by getting into an argument the teenager gets some of what he or she wants—they establish standing in the process of disagreement before consent is given. This is one compromise you can make to encourage teenage compliance. After you have heard his objections out, after he has put up a self-respecting amount of resistance, he goes along with what you asked.

2. *Insistence* is the power of pursuit. "I will keep after you and after you and after you about this until you do what I ask." A father uses insistence to wear teenage resistance down, the young person finally giving consent to get the father off her

case. "I finally picked up my dirty clothes because I got tired of my dad hassling me about it!" Teenagers know relentless insistence works because they often use it to wear parental resistance down, turning an initial "No" into an ultimate "Yes." "All right, you can have some gas money, just stop asking me about it!"

Insistence is nagging, and nagging is honorable—albeit exhausting—work. It needs to be done. It shows a father is sufficiently serious about a request to relentlessly pursue the teenager until it is finally accomplished. Since nagging is the drudge work of parenting, if there are two parents it needs to be shared, otherwise one parent will appear "mean" and the other not, an unfair distinction that can become divisive in the relationship. To give many mothers their due, they tend to be much more faithful naggers than fathers, who have far less tolerance for this onerous work and tend to cede it to their wives, abandon pursuit, or move on to threat of punishment if teenage consent is not quickly given. Nagging takes patience and persistence, and it is a good discipline strategy for you to learn.

Insistence is too important to mix with anger because becoming emotionally upset only ends up empowering the teenager. When the parent loses control to get control the teenager ends up in control. "When I have to ask you again and again and again to get something done, you make me so angry!" only communicates that the teenager has been given power to provoke this emotion in his father. Who's in the position of authority now? The message insistence needs to send is one of unwavering resolution: "I won't let up or give up about this until you get it done." Therefore, if nagging starts to frustrate you, and frustration starts to lead you to anger, just call a time out, separate, cool down, and then engage in the discussion once more.

3. *Reprisal* is the power of punishment. To show he means what he says, a father should not promise consequences he is not prepared to carry out. An empty threat is an expression of desperation at best and impotence at worst. Your punishment says: "In consequence of violating a major family rule, there is a penalty you must pay." This is why a father needs

to avoid punishing in anger. An angry father is likely to decree an unrealistic punishment ("You're grounded for the next year!") and then have to retract and modify the penalty once he has calmed down, thereby communicating inconsistency. In addition, he needs to separate any expression of anger from deciding on a punishment, or else the teenager will think she is only being punished because the father is angry, and so she misses understanding the connection between offense and consequence.

The purpose of punishment is simply to apply a consequence that may cause the child to rethink an infraction and consent to not repeat it again. If a father is upset over the violation that has occurred, he should share his feelings with his teenager: "I'm really angry that you stole and used my credit card!" Then he should delay consideration of punishment until he can make a reasonable and appropriately selected consequence, "When I've had a chance to think about it, then I'll tell you what you need to do!" Inadvertently, the father has applied a double punishment, the teenager hating worst of all having to wait and to discover his payment due.

The most common punishment chosen with an adolescent is usually deprivation, taking away some freedom, like social contact, use of the car, or access to electronic communication or entertainment. Kept short term, deprivation can make a symbolic point, but in the extreme it is risky. Strip a teenager of all desirable freedoms (as anger can cause a father to impulsively do) and the teen triumphantly declares: "Now I have nothing left to lose 'cause you've got nothing left to take way!" At worst, protracted grounding (several months of social isolation) can create a depth of hurt and unforgiving anger that may set the teenager on a revengeful path: "I'll hurt myself to hurt you like you've hurt me!" Where does a father go from here?

The man would have been better off using a more powerful punishment than deprivation: *reparation*. "As a result of breaking the rules, you have to do additional household tasks to work the violation off, work that must be accomplished before you get to do anything else you want." The father asserts far more authority with reparation because doing work for him requires more energy than simply doing without.

In general, reparation is more successful with a willful child than deprivation, which only heightens frustration and increases anger. The reason parents don't like using reparation is that it takes supervision. It feels easier just to take something away. Deprivation is easier than reparation, but it is far less effective.

Of course, the most powerful punishment, the one most teenagers hate worse than either deprivation or reparation, is communication in the form of a "good talking to." "A bad talking to, you mean," objects the teenager. "I hate lectures!" To which the father replies: "You need to know that any time you choose to operate outside of family rules, the first thing that's going to happen is always going to be communication. You will sit down and sit still until I have told you everything I have to say on the subject of your offense, *and* until I am told by you everything I want to hear about what happened, why it happened, and how it's not going to happen again. You will not only have to listen to me, but you will have to talk to me. How long this conversation goes on will depend not just on your having heard enough from me, but also on me having heard enough from you. Then I will decide what further consequence may be imposed." Often quick to take action and go right from infraction to punishment, many fathers are not as well versed in giving lectures as mothers. However, this is an important skill for a father to learn since teenagers usually consider it the most onerous consequence of all.

Finally, a father needs to maintain the distinction between dealing with aggravating resistance (continually delaying doing chores, leaving a mess, playing music too loud) and dealing with unacceptable violations (sneaking out after hours, lying about what happened, keeping illegal substances in the home).

Think about a father who, in anger at small offenses, cannot keep this distinction clear. Frustration getting the better of him, he grounds his daughter for a month for once again leaving the refrigerator ajar and water running in the kitchen sink. "How many times have I told you!" he screams. But what is this man going to do when, later that week, she sneaks out, unlicensed and with a neighbor friend, to take a 2:00 A.M. joy ride in the family car, and the father has just used his big gun on punishing a kitchen mess?

Use insistence to deal with delayed compliance and normal adolescent irritations; use reprisal to deal with major rule violations. Chores are a supervisory issue; punishment is reserved for significant infractions. And beware the influence of your anger. It can cause you to over-punish to harmful effect. Punishment with the verbal or emotional or physical intent to do injury (demeaning your teenager or inflicting bodily pain) risks having a damaging effect upon the relationship, building grievance, resentment, and humiliation in your teenager rather than a healthy respect for your authority.

4. *Fair exchange* is the power to exploit the teenager's dependence on you to satisfy her many lifestyle needs. The watchword here is: *no automatic giving.* Any time your teenager asks for anything, first ask yourself: Was there something I asked this young person for that has not yet been delivered, or is there some help I would like from this young person? Use the leverage of her dependency on you to get before you give. "I would be happy to do what you ask, but before I do, I want something from you first."

Teenagers continually rely on you for all kinds of basic support: meals and transportation, TV and computer use, money, and for permissions (like to have friends over). Each occasion of need or want is a fair exchange point that a father can use if compliance with some previous request has not been met. "I'd be happy to drive you to the store, but first pick up your dirty laundry like I asked." Replies the teenager: "I promise I will when we get back." No. Promises are false currency with resistant teenagers who have not proved to be true to their word before. Now, only performance counts. The father withholds what the teenager wants until consent to a previous request has been given: "Let me know when I can see the laundry has been picked up, and then we can go."

Also at issue here is the opportunity for the father to teach the principle of mutuality. "Family relationships must be conducted to meet needs of both parties, not just one." A father who does not encourage his teenagers to live in two-way relationships (each party giving to and doing for the other) often ends up resenting a son or daughter who acts like his or her own needs are the only ones that matter. Even worse, the man sends out into the world a "spoiled" young person who is too self-centered for his or her own good, and who painfully discovers that what the father indulgently allowed, other people will not tolerate. Spoiled for healthy relationships is the unhappy outcome, at least until the young person learns to correct the self-centered error of his or her ways.

5. *Appreciation* is the power of approval: "Thank you for picking up your room." Even if it has taken a steadfast father two hours of explanation, insistence, and working the fair exchange to get a ten-minute task accomplished, the exhausted man needs to thank the child for compliance. Otherwise, the teenager will complain about what is often true: "You never appreciate what I do!" A father should always reward compliance with appreciation because by doing so he encourages further consent.

If you want to shape desirable behavior, rewarding the good with positive attention is infinitely more powerful than punishing the bad with a negative consequence because teenagers are more motivated by seeking pleasure than they are by avoiding pain. Even sullen adolescents, who act like parental opinion doesn't matter, would rather please their parents than not. A father's good opinion can count for a lot.

With a toddler, a father naturally uses his power of approval to shape behavior, but with a teenager, because of all the new aggravations, he tends to forget. A more critical response to more resistant circumstances feels natural, but it is ill advised because positive attention is still the greatest influence he has. As mentioned before, it is through investing positive attention in his teenager that a father increases the likelihood of receiving a positive and cooperative return. One positive return, however, that becomes increasingly hard for a father to get during adolescence is the teenager's sincere apology for having done wrong.

THE PROBLEM OF REMORSE

At such a self-centering period of growth, it is easy for teenagers to act unmindfully and inconsiderately of others, impulsively and thoughtlessly giving offense or committing injury in the process of going after what they want or don't want to happen. So a younger sibling is in tears because a teenage sister, impatient to escape her bad day at school, grabs the remote from the child who's watching a favorite TV show and switches the channel to suit her older tastes. Reprimanded by her father, the teenager throws down the remote and stalks out of the room, angrily dismissing her sister's upset, "Oh let the little baby have her way!" The man comforts his younger daughter and then pursues his older one, unwilling to let this insensitive and high-handed behavior go. "I want you to go right back and tell your sister you're sorry for what you did!" He thinks his older daughter should apologize for doing hurt, when the only thing she's really sorry for is getting caught in the act of misbehavior and getting reprimanded for it. *True remorse is in short supply in adolescence.*

Suppose you were in this man's place, what else might you do? In your role as parental authority you could do this. You could realize that although forced apology has no remorseful value, there are two responses that may cause your teenage daughter to think more deeply about what she did—empathy and amends. So in service of empathy, you require your daughter to engage in this exercise: "Tell me three ways you would feel if what you did to your sister had been done to you." And in service of amends: "Tell me what action you're going to take to make up to your sister for the injury you gave."

KEEPING PARENTAL INFLUENCE IN PERSPECTIVE

Adolescence teaches most fathers a lesson in humility. When your children were very young you may have had large ambitions for your parental influence, believing it would be largely responsible for shaping how they grew into young adults. But their adolescence teaches you to know better, to put your parental influence in perspective. Now you can see it as only one of a multiplicity of influences that determine how your teenagers will grow and ultimately turn out. You have no control over these other influences

You don't control the larger culture and the onslaught of media messages that it sends—the experiences it glamorizes, the ideals it presents, and the motivations it encourages. You don't control your teenager's inborn characteristics—the temperament, personality, and aptitudes that genetic inheritance endows. You don't control the choices your teenager makes—you can inform those choices, but final decisions are up to the adolescent. You don't control the circumstances to which your child is exposed away from home—the unfamiliar and challenging situations your teenager gets into out in the world. You don't control the teenager's companions and the pressures they can bring to bear—inviting opportunities for risk taking, for experimenting with adventure and the forbidden. And you don't control chance events—how luck can spare or victimize a young person's life.

You need to keep this perspective in mind when conduct of your teenager's life is not going well. For you to attribute what is happening (substance abuse, for example) or what is not happening (maintaining grades commensurate with ability, for example) to your parenting credits the power of your influence too much. It also creates an unhealthy opening for your errant teenager to cast off honest responsibility with dishonest blame. "You're right," agrees your middle-school child, "if you hadn't changed jobs and moved where we lived and made me go to a new school, my grades wouldn't have dropped the way they have!" No. The current failure is from failing effort, not from new surroundings, and you must hold the young person to this honest account.

As a parent, you need to limit your sense of responsibility; but you cannot do this without acknowledging the limits of your authority as well. Here are some limitations you may not like, but must accept. As a father, you cannot fully protect your teenagers from harm any more than you can fully prepare them for the future. You can be right some of the time about what is best for them, but you cannot be right all of the time. You can know a lot about life, but you cannot always know what to do. You can give a full-faith fathering effort, but you cannot always get the outcome you desire.

A father who assumes responsibility for everything that happens to his child becomes bound by a false equation: parents = child. This linkage ties adequacy of parenting to performance of the child, how well or badly a child does becoming a measure of the parenting received. Bound by this belief, when the child makes a bad choice, a father feels impelled to fault himself: "What have I done wrong?" Better for him to break this equation and maintain a realistic perspective instead: "As a good father, I have good teenagers who will sometimes make bad choices in the normal trial-and-error process of growing up. A bad choice does not make a bad teenager any more than a bad-acting teenager makes me a bad father."

Parenting is only one small influence among many that shape a child's and teenager's growth. The limit of your authority and the power of your parental influence comes down to this: the example that you model (who and how you are) and the parental treatment you provide (how you choose to act and react with your adolescents). Accept your parental limitations, humble your authority, and you may reduce the likelihood of your anger.

AUTHORITY AND ANGER

Many fathers would have considerably less anger to contend with if they could sacrifice a measure of pride in their authority and learn to act with more humility around the issue of control. As a performance person and a performance parent, pride in your authority can set you up for disappointment come your children's adolescence. As your traditional standing is harder to maintain, and in defense of declining authority, you may resort to anger to protest the loss and get your way. When you do, your teenagers start to wonder what happened to their dad. Why are you so mad all the time? They don't see how they are frustrating your need for pride:

- to be in charge,
- to be right,
- to be the expert,
- to be agreed with,
- to be obeyed and not delayed,
- to have the last word,
- to be above criticism,
- to be deferred to,
- to win arguments at all costs,
- to never admit being wrong,
- to never apologize.

Pride of this kind is about preserving and saving face, maintaining dominance as a parent, which becomes harder to do when children enter adolescence and tend either to discount or take on their father's authority. At such times, it's easy to rise to your own defense: "I'm still your father, and you will do what I say!" And now a father is willing to do battle with his belligerent teenage son to show the adolescent who is still man of the house, who makes the rules, who *will* be obeyed: "I'll show you who's boss!" Talk about a losing proposition!

The lesson is that anger in defense of pride does not work well. Humility works best, accepting that as adolescents grow in self-determination, the father necessarily loses some traditional parental influence and standing, even though as a connected father you continue to take responsible stands. Remember, this is how growing up is supposed to be: The teenager gathers power of independence as parents let go of some control until he is finally ready to step off on his own.

So beware.

- A father with a low tolerance for delay can be at high risk for *irritation.*
- A father with a low tolerance for argument can be at high risk for *temper.*
- A father with a low tolerance for defiance can be at high risk for *abuse.*

WHO IS IN CHARGE OF THE FATHER'S ANGER?

Does this sound familiar?

"My teenager gets me angry!"
"My teenager makes me so upset!"
"My teenager made me lose my temper!"

Wrong, wrong, wrong. How the teenager acts is up to the teenager. How the father chooses to feel in response is up to the father. When a father gives up responsibility for his emotional state by blaming his teenager for causing it, he gives that young person far too much power. Believing that the teenager is in charge of the father's feelings, the father now gets really angry with the teenager for "controlling" the man's emotions. The law of psychological responsibility is simply this: Each individual (and no one else) decides how he or she is going to feel, think, and act.

Anger is a feeling, and like all emotions it is functional. Emotions operate like an early awareness system. They catch and direct our attention to something important going on in our psychological world. Emotions are informants. Positively experienced emotions bring welcome news. Joy is about fulfillment. Pride is about accomplishment. Gratitude is about appreciation.

Negatively experienced emotions bring undesirable news. Fear alerts us to danger. Frustration identifies blockage. And *anger patrols violations to our well-being*. What kind of violations? There are many kinds. There is anger at wrongdoing, at unfairness, at betrayal, at mistreatment, at broken agreements.

Having directed a man's attention to some violation, anger empowers an expressive, protective, or corrective response. So in response to his frustrated teenager's insulting language ("Dad, you're such a *jerk!*") a father replies: "Don't put me down with sarcasm by calling me a demeaning name. As your parent, it hurts me when you do. I don't speak to you that way, and I don't want to be spoken to that way again."

The quality of communication is the quality of family life, and name-calling is doubly destructive communication. Bad names are used both to injure with insults and to justify mistreatment. Having called his father a "jerk," now the son may feel entitled to treat (mistreat) his dad. Remember, in an extreme example, all hate crimes are preceded by name-calling. So: Neither employ nor allow it in your home.

Being able to use anger to patrol personal well-being for violations is important, like the dad calling his son on the use of insulting speech. But anger must be used constructively, not destructively, and the father needs to lead by example. So:

- *Declare it:* "I am feeling angry."
- *Direct it:* "I think what you did (or didn't do) is wrong."
- *Defuse it:* "This is what needs to happen for me to let my anger go."

To the son who used sarcasm and name-calling, the father might additionally want to say something like this: "There's no way that my authority as your father is sometimes not going to cause you to feel anger at me. When this occurs, you need to know that I am always willing to hear your frustration with me, what I did or didn't do, and try to talk it through. Even though I may not change my mind, I want you to have your say so at least I understand how you feel. Part of my job as your dad is to make sure that rules for safe communication are followed in the family. One of those rules is that anger is never allowed to serve as an excuse for doing anyone impulsive or intentional harm."

Unfortunately, a father coming out of an abusive family background is at risk of mishandling anger in two ways with his provocative adolescents. If he *adjusted* to abusive parents by not objecting, taking what was given, being too frightened to say anything lest he make a bad situation worse, he may have ended up with an incapacity for feeling or expressing anger, no matter what mistreatment he receives. So when his teenagers cross the line of acceptable behavior into hurtful behavior, he is prone to let mistreatment get worse. If the father *identified* with the abusive behavior of his parents, however, learning that anger can empower verbal or physical violence to take control and that that's okay, then he may imitate their abusive ways when he feels crossed by his adolescents, inflicting injury to everyone's cost, to victim and witnesses.

ANGER AND VIOLENCE

Social and domestic violence is disproportionately a male problem. Anger is the usual precursor for violent behavior because it provides two kinds of motivation at once. It provides emotional motivation, the intensity from feeling upset and aroused; and it provides intellectual motivation, the justification from believing one has been wronged or treated unfairly. Together the two motivations encourage striking back or striking out. So anger is a risk factor in violence.

As a father, your job is to express your anger in a manner that feels safe for everyone in the family. Of course, there are some fathers who disagree with this objective: "It's okay that my kids don't like my anger if it causes them to do what I say. It makes them *respect* my authority."

Not exactly. Actually, if they fear their father's anger, that can make them have *contempt* for his authority, as one teenage daughter privately confessed. "Dad's nothing but a bully! He uses his anger to scare us into doing what he wants. He gets all red in the face. His eyes get wide. His mouth snarls up. I mean he looks like he's about to go crazy and do something awful. That's why we all back down and stay out of his way."

The cost of fear-based authority like this is loss of trust, closeness, and honest communication from the people the father loves. Now his children smile to his face and complain about him behind his back. They keep their distance, carefully craft what they have to say, and learn to be dishonest to keep him ignorant about what they are really feeling, about what is really going on. In many cases like this that I have seen, the father in question tends to discount the influence of his anger.

"I don't know what you're talking about," protests the dad. "I suppose I do look angry when I get angry, but so what? I don't know what they're afraid of. It's not like I'd ever hit anybody. I've never done that." In counseling, I give the man a pocket mirror so that he can see what his children see when he gets angry. "This next week," I suggest, "whenever you get angry at any of them, immediately get off by yourself and look at your face in the mirror. Next session, come back and tell me what you've seen." Most fathers come back the following week sobered by what they saw. "I guess I do look fearsome. It reminds me of how my dad used to look to me. You know, I never wanted to have my kids frightened of me the way I was of him. I can't believe I turned out like this. I need to make some changes."

Family violence need only happen once to leave lasting instability, something a father may find hard to accept. "I don't understand it," he complained. "That was eight years ago. My wife mouthed off and criticized my kicking back after a long day at work and without thinking I threw my drink at her and the glass shattered on the wall. Of course, I've never gotten physically angry again, but no one in the family is willing to forget. What's the matter with them anyway?" The matter is that a single episode of angry violence is enough to frighten a family about if and when it might happen again. As stated by the Alabama Coalition against Domestic Violence (see www.acadv.org, 12/10/06), "family violence creates a home environment where children live in constant fear."

A father should express his anger in a safe and constructive way, appropriate for dealing with the violation that occurred. "When you took what was mine without asking, and returned it broken, I felt really angry! Now I need to know how you are planning to make it up to me." If you're too angry to discuss what happened right away, take a time out before you talk, take a walk, go to the gym, or, to focus your feelings, even take the time to write your feelings out.

In our society, it is often assumed that men are more comfortable with anger because it's associated with being tough, combative, forceful, and even fierce, the types of traits we often ascribe to male action heroes. Anger means a man won't take mistreatment, will stand up for himself, will defend and protect his own, won't back down, is not afraid to fight, will even vow revenge. Anger overrides other emotions and energizes aggression. When men feel angry they feel strong, and when they act angry they look manly (at least that's what they believe). Most important, anger can be a cover emotion for many men. Beneath its aggressive shield are often more vulnerable emotions—for example, hurt, fear, disappointment, humiliation, failure, guilt, and shame—that may be kept hidden or denied. This is why, when a father gets angry, he needs to stop and think and ask himself the clarifying question: "Besides anger, what else might I be feeling, and how can I let other people know?"

WHEN A MAN IS ANGER PRONE

What if you are susceptible to violations and quick to anger most of the time? Given that your children's adolescence can be a very provocative age, what can you do to reduce your readiness to take offense? First, consider three common predispositions to anger.

1. A father who has a *high need for control* will often get mad when he doesn't get his way or doesn't get what he wants right away. Because adolescents tend to become more passively resistant as well as actively challenging, a father with a low tolerance for delay and defiance can be at higher *risk for angry abuse*—losing his temper to get control.
2. A father who is *highly judgmental* will often get angry when others contradict or disagree with his opinions or don't follow

what he considers the "right" way. Because adolescents tend to become rebelliously concerned with embracing an independent set of values, a father with a low tolerance for diversity is at higher *risk for angry sarcasm*—putting down and cutting down beliefs he won't allow.

3. A father who has a *high sensitivity to insult* will often get angry when he takes frustrating or offensive incidents personally, though they were not meant that way. Because adolescents tend to become more self-preoccupied and less considerate, a father who is vulnerable to slights is at higher *risk for feeling attacked and angrily retaliating* by interpreting ignorant or insensitive affronts as acts of deliberate intent.

Fathers can reduce this susceptibility by regularly repeating to themselves corrective messages. By changing how you think, you can change how you feel.

1. To be less controlling, practice saying: "To be okay, I don't have to have everything go my way."
2. To be less judgmental, practice saying: "I don't have to be right about everything or have everything done 'right.'"
3. To be less sensitive to hurt, practice saying: "Just because I don't like how someone acts doesn't mean that person is out to get me."

And if you are prone not just to getting angry, but to *staying* angry, holding on to grievances rather than letting them go, beware how you may hurt family relationships and yourself. Your anger disconnects you from those you love, who may seek safety in physical and emotional distance. Toward others this well of anger is likely to seep out in small expressions and acts of hostility, like sarcasm and deliberate discourtesy. Within yourself you can create an unhappy living condition, resentment, that can cause you to feel "angry all the time." If this emotional state describes you, consider an aphorism from Alcoholics Anonymous: "Resentment is like taking poison and waiting for the other person to die." You may want to get some help to stop poisoning yourself.

In *Beyond Anger: A Guide for Men,* Thomas Harbin reports: "If you look at the families of angry men, you'll find that they often include fathers, grandfathers, uncles, and brothers who are angry too. To a large degree, angry men have been conditioned to act this way." He goes on to counsel: "The feelings that lead to anger need to be expressed. You must learn to identify your frustration, humiliation, and worry; acknowledge these feelings to yourself and others; and deal with the circumstances producing these emotions before you get angry. For most angry men, expressing their anger only produces more anger.... The big step in controlling your angry responses is to anticipate anger-provoking situations and make plans to deal with them before they happen." (See Harbin, 2000.)

Anger is a good servant, but a bad master. If you are a father who is anger prone, practice changing your mental sets to reduce your susceptibility to anger. People who think with their feelings, particularly their feelings of anger, do so at their own and other people's costs. If you feel anger, delay action until you have had time to think. Model the use of anger that you want your children to learn, declaring it in a safe and non-abusive manner. In addition, if alcohol brings out your anger, your more irritable or hostile side that sobriety keeps under safe restraint, then for the sake of your love of family and for your family's love for you, do everyone a favor. Don't drink.

THE WAY IT IS

Come your children's adolescence,

- Your authority will be more frequently challenged,
- Your power will be more frequently diminished,
- Your pride will be more frequently offended,
- Your anger will be more frequently aroused.

As a father, you need to know that it is perfectly okay to feel anger and to declare anger, but it is *not* okay to let your anger do any family member harm. Assert or defend your authority with anger, and you and the adolescent may regret impulsive words you say or harsh actions that you take.

CHAPTER TEN

CONDUCTING COMMUNICATION

Quality of family life has a lot to do with quality of family communication, with how and how well people get along. Family members depend on the adequate, accurate, and respectful exchange of information to stay securely connected with each other. Communication is a lifeline that allows family members to know what's happening in each other's lives, to be sensitive to each other's needs, to disclose thoughts and feelings, to be supportive of each other when hard times hit, and to get questions asked and answered.

It is the rule, not the exception, that come adolescence your teenager is going to become *less* inclined to talk with you. More social separation, more desire for privacy and independence, more sense of the intergenerational differences between you, more distrust of your authority, all conspire to create less desire to share. However, just because your teenager is less communicative with you is no reason for you to be less communicative with him or her. In fact, your job as a father is to keep up the communication initiative, to create opportunities for ongoing talk to keep you both informed about what's going on with each other, to keep you connected.

The key principle for inviting communication from your adolescent is *accessibility*—at any time, no matter how inconvenient, being willing to listen to your teenager when he or she wants to talk with you. Sometimes a father has to learn this principle the hard way.

For example, a dad who is too busy, is watching TV, is wanting to relax, is wanting to be left alone, is feeling too tired, or is simply not in a listening mood will put off a teenage invitation to talk until "later," only to discover that "later" never comes. Now his teenager no longer feels like talking because the readiness to talk with his dad is fleeting. A lot of conditions have to come together for the teenager to want to initiate significant conversation with his dad—trust in the relationship, lack of personal distraction, desire to be known, emotional comfort, and who knows what else. An opening for communication can quickly close if not immediately seized when offered. Fathers mistakenly believe offers to talk are for "now or later," when for the adolescent it is "now or never." Next time a teenage invitation to talk comes your way, interrupt what you're doing, or delay what you were going to do, and welcome with interest this chance to hear what's on the teenager's mind. Make the effort to communicate.

When the challenging adolescent years arrive, *what* difficulties a father goes through with his teenagers can be less important to the well-being of their relationship than *how* they go through it together, and that *how* is communication. Failure to communicate (particularly during challenge, change, conflict, or crisis) is why many committed fathers end up estranged from their teenagers. However, sometimes just talking to each other is complicated by a set of problems that makes it far from easy.

A SIMPLE PSYCHOLOGY OF COMMUNICATION

What is communication? Think of it this way. Suppose the two of you, father and adolescent, are talking face to face and you ask your teenager three simple questions, the answers to which will yield some basic information about your state of being.

- "What am I *feeling* right now?"
- "What am I *thinking* right now?"
- "What was I *doing* when you were at school today?"

Simple questions for you to ask can be impossible for your teenager to accurately answer. For your teenager to truly know the answers to these questions, you must disclose this information because this data is yours alone to share or to withhold. *When it comes to what you are feeling, thinking, and doing, you control the power to be known.* Reverse the situation, and have your teenager ask the same three questions of you. Now the power to be known is up to him or her.

Since each individual is the ultimate authority on his or her own experience, no one can know that person's inner workings or worldly doings without that person communicating what is going on. Without being told, other people must intuit the individual's feelings and thoughts, or must depend on hearsay. So, the realities upon which family communication depends are difficult because:

- To a large degree, we are all strangers, even to those we know and love the best;
- How well we know each other depends on what we each choose to disclose;
- There is no mind reading, only guessing;
- To stay current with each other, we must be regularly informed;
- Ignorance of each other is what communication strives to overcome;
- Sending and receiving information about our feelings, thoughts, and behaviors is how verbal communication helps keep us connected;
- Inadequate sharing of data in relationships can be hurtful: Ignorance can breed estrangement, distrust, anxiety, loneliness, projection, rejection, and isolation.

Add all these hard realities up, and it should give you incentive as a father to do all you can to create a relationship with your teenager in which ongoing, adequate, and accurate information is mutually sent and received. *To stay connected with your teenagers, data about feelings, thoughts, and behaviors must be shared on a regular basis.*

FEELING CUT OFF

For the most part, verbal communication about what is happening keeps you and your teenager adequately informed and closely connected. Stop the flow of information, shut down the exchange of vital data, and both of you will feel cut off from each other. However, trying to prime the flow of information with questions to show your interest and curiosity is often counterproductive. Here's a situation that may be familiar to you.

"My teenager won't talk to me, won't tell me about her life, won't share about herself no matter how many questions I ask!" For the father in this situation, questions seem like a logical way to open up the flow of communication from his daughter, but she sees it differently. "I hate the way he pries!" The dad believes he is inviting conversation when he is actually shutting it down, not understanding that at this stage of teenage life his questions are offensive. They are emblematic of his authority and they are invasive of her privacy, two very sensitive issues to most teenagers. What can he do? He could choose to model the kind of sharing he would like from his teenager by sharing about himself—what he did in his past life or what his daily experience is like. If all he is willing to do is talk about her, he will turn her off because an information imbalance is created. Teenagers tend to become uncommunicative with a father who only wants to talk about them, and never about himself.

In addition, her father could also declare his information needs without asking questions that his teenager often finds offensive. He could make a request, he could ask for help, and he could make a statement of need. The first strategy honors her right to share or not to share, the second strategy petitions her assistance, and the third strategy declares what it feels like for him *not* to know.

> *The request statement* is: "I would really value knowing a little
>   more about what is going on."
> *The help statement is:* "Could you help me better understand
>   what is happening?"
> *The need statement* is: "It would really ease my mind to have
>   some information to reduce my fears."

In return, the father needs to express appreciation for the information she provides, and for the sense of connection it creates. Notice that none of his three statements are emblematic of his authority or demandingly invasive of her privacy. They all respect the fact that communication is up to her.

The very private and uncommunicative father who complains that his teenagers won't communicate with him may want to look at the example that he sets. Often, he only has himself to blame. He has to train himself to become a personally expressive and forthright communicator if he wants to stay informed by, and connected to, his adolescents.

The non-communicative father, by not talking about himself, cuts his teenagers off from a very powerful and important source of education. What a father primarily gives his children is the person he is—not just a dad to interact with, but someone to get to know. This knowledge includes information about his background, journey through life, and what he has learned along the way. In addition, he is a link in the chain of generations, an invaluable informant about memories he has and stories he's been told about his forbears that create a precious sense of connection between his teenagers and their extended family history.

Sometimes in counseling I ask an older adolescent to tell me about her father, and very commonly this is the response I get: "I can't tell you much. I don't know him that well. Mostly all we've ever talked about is me." What a loss! What a waste! She has been denied learning about the life experience of her father. He apparently thought that fathering meant keeping the parental focus of conversation on and about her, and off him. It's a complimentary belief to the old notion that "a child should be seen but not heard," only it's "a father should know but not be known." A lot of "distant fathers" are distant not because they are physically absent, but because they are unwilling to share about themselves with their kids. It's best to be a father your children and teenagers are invited to know.

Of course, what parts of your past you wish to keep private from your teenagers is always up to you. No parent is completely open to children about everything, nor should they be. However, what about when, from his adventurous, illegal, or painful personal experience in high school, a father learned some dangerous lessons about life that his teenager, by being told, might choose to avoid?

Consider one topic of sharing that many fathers find controversial and refuse to discuss—their own history of substance use. Now that his freshman in high school is bringing stories home about what older students like to do when skipping school, or after school, or at parties, it's time for her father, if he hasn't already done so, to normalize discussion of substance use. His job is not to condemn what she describes, it's to inform her understanding and perhaps influence her choices by sharing what he knows about the risks involved. But when prompted in counseling to share some of his substance experience with her, he is outraged: "Are you crazy! Why that would be like giving her permission to use, even encouragement. 'Well, if you drank growing up, why shouldn't I?' she'd say."

But I disagree. He can become a very credible informant should he choose to share his own experience. If he has never used substances, he can explain why, and he can share cautionary stories about friends who got hurt when they did. He can share information about people in the extended family history who may have had, or now have, problems with alcohol or other drugs, and the troubles they have caused. People she knows and can relate to in the family often provide real-life examples she can identify with and learn from.

If sharing your own substance use history feels risky, moderate the risk by contracting for a fair exchange of data. Tell her you will answer any questions she has about your history of use so she can learn from your experience, knowledge, and mistakes, *assuming* she will agree to answer with equal honesty questions about her own exposure to, and experiences with, substances. Of course, you are *not* giving her your blessing to use. You don't want her to use because it increases so many other adolescent risks for getting hurt—car accidents, physical violence, and sexual exploitation. Your prohibition, however, does not provide protection enough because it does not prepare her for safe and knowledgeable use when, sooner or later, the decision to experiment or recreationally use is made. As a responsible father raising teenagers in a drug-filled world, you *must* communicate and connect about the issue of substance use. Sharing about your own history increases the credibility of what you have to say.

As her dad, ask yourself a simple question: "Are there any lessons from my own history of substance use or experience with others that could inform and perhaps protect my teenager if he or she was told?" If so, give your teenagers the benefit of your experience and share what you know. Here's an example. A father with many years of recovery in AA had this to share: "I know this much from my own bad experience with alcohol: Excessive drinking got me in trouble in at least four ways. When I had a problem, rather than face it, I'd drink to avoid it. Instead of doing what was important for my future, I'd lose myself in what felt good in the present. Instead of behaving responsibly, I'd act like I didn't care. And instead of being honest about what was going on, I'd lie about it to myself and others to get by."

Some of the best substance abuse prevention parenting comes from fathers in recovery who cite chapter and verse from their own painful experience to help teenagers follow an abstinent or moderate way.

DISCONNECTORS

The cardinal sin of communication is *lying,* deliberately falsifying information. It causes the person lied to to feel fooled and mislead, frightened and hurt, angry and betrayed when dishonesty is discovered: "How can I trust you when you won't trust me with the truth?" Father and teenager must rely on the validity of each other's information about their lives to be adequately and accurately informed. Trust, security, and intimacy are at stake. *There is no trust without truth, there is no security without sincerity, and there is no intimacy without honesty.*

As mentioned earlier in the chapter on mid-adolescence, a father needs to be more than a truth-teller with his teenager; he must hold that young person to honest account and take lying very seriously. When an act of deceit occurs, he must:

- Fully explain what it feels like to be lied to (lies have emotional impact);
- Get a full explanation for why the lie occurred (lying is intentional, motivated by cause);
- Get the teenager's commitment not to lie again (giving a word to be trusted);
- Apply some task of reparation around the home (working the lie off);
- Reinstate the expectation for honesty (in a healthy relationship, truth telling must be assumed).

Next time a lie is found out, remember that there is a longer-term issue to be addressed. If lies are ignored, they will be relied on to avoid accountability in future relationships, usually to the young adult's cost. So the father can truly say: "I am acting to discourage your lying now not just for me and for us, but for you, so you do not get in the habit of lying to others later on." As a father, take a stand for sharing honest information, for telling the truth.

And if you are a very strict, critical or intimidating father, be on the watch for two kinds of teenage lies. For the sake of avoiding conflict, your teenager may placate you by saying what you want to hear, and for the sake of gaining approval, your teenager may try to please you by saying what you want to hear. If you suspect either lie, you may want to consider softening your authority and becoming more reasonable and affirming to work with.

Come adolescence, lying tends to increase when the young person desires freedom outside of what parents will allow, or wants to escape losing freedom for misbehavior. Seeing his ten-year-old beginning to venture down this path of small deceits, a father at a workshop described an object lesson he created to teach his daughter what the father's words had failed to convey. One day he said to his daughter: "Just so you know, sometime in the next two weeks I'm going to tell you a really big lie." "You wouldn't lie to me," replied his daughter. "You don't believe in lying, you've told me so." "None the less," answered the dad, "in the next two weeks I'm going to tell you a lie." So the daughter watched, waited, and wondered. "Permission to sleep over this weekend, is that the lie?" she wanted to know. "No, that's not the lie," reassured the dad. Later, the daughter asks: "Being allowed to get the CD with what I've worked to earn, is that the lie?" "No," says the dad, "you earned the money." "Being able to take dance lessons, is that it, is that the lie?" Now the daughter was feeling frantic to know. "No," says the dad, "that's not the lie." And finally the two weeks were up. "Where's the lie?" asked the daughter. "You said I could expect a lie!" "That's right," said the dad. "That was the lie. That's how it feels to be lied to." And from that simple object lesson, the precocious only child at age ten learned a life lesson from her dad about the emotional power of lies.

Of course, like any teenager, when it comes to telling the truth by sharing adequate and accurate information, even this young woman will increasingly find herself on the horns of a dilemma. Honest disclosure about everything she has done, is doing, or is wanting to do, while maintaining truthful standing with her father, may also cause him to punish her for some of her past actions, limit some of her present activities, and forbid some of her future plans. So honesty becomes a compromise as she elects to mostly, but not always, tell the truth to her dad, just like he compromised when being honest as a teenager with parents of his own. Like most teenagers, she will behave partly within and partly outside his rules, and she will tell him some of the truth, but not all of it, much of the time.

THE ROLES OF TALKER AND LISTENER

Father and teenager both need to contribute to a strong connection by talking and listening. To have one person who does all the talking and rarely listens, and another person who does all the listening and rarely talks, can create an awkward situation. The sharer may complain: "You never say anything." The listener may complain: "When I do you act uninterested and impatient, or interrupt me!"

Capacities for both talking and listening are required for adequate communication to happen. So as a father, check yourself out. If you're a lecturer who doesn't listen, or a listener who doesn't like to talk, for the sake of connecting with your teenager, mend your one-sided ways and be a sender and a receiver of data, a talker and a listener. If you're a man who is used to dictating the course and content of conversation, has a hard time listening when you disagree, and finds it difficult attending to what doesn't interest you and being patient to hear the other person out, then you need to correct your habits of communication. If you're a man who is by nature shy or reserved, unpracticed or uncomfortable talking about yourself, or believes your opinions and beliefs should be private, you need to correct these habits as well. *What you model is what you teach.*

Consider the following example of what can happen when a father routinely doesn't attend what his daughter has to say. "I don't know why my daughter gets so upset when I don't listen to her, why she makes it such a big deal. Sometimes I'm tired. Sometimes I've got other things on my mind." His daughter helps him understand: "When you don't listen to me, what you are showing is that I'm not *worth* listening to, and that really hurts my feelings! I feel put down!" Repeatedly not listening to a family member who has something important to say can feel abusive.

ELECTRONIC INTERFERENCE

Information technology has enriched and complicated our lives in extraordinary ways. On the one hand, e-mail, cell phones, instant messaging, and the like all provide ways for people to connect at a distance. On the other hand, those devices also provide a level of electronic interference that can interfere with communication at home. One study of the change in family communication wrought by our information age noted that "greater use of the Internet was associated with declines in participants' communication with family members in the household." (See Kraut, Patterson, Lundmark et al. in *American Psychologist*, vol. 53, 1998.)

How is a father supposed to have meaningful talk with a teenager when she's either on her cell phone, on the computer, listening to loud music, ear-plugged into a portable entertainment center, or watching TV? How is he supposed to break through all that electronic interference and connect? Whatever happened to the days of people giving each other undivided attention when there was something important to say? What happened to casual conversation with each other?

Getting that dedicated quality of in-person contact between parent and adolescent is definitely more complex than it used to be because of the competing channels of communication on which the teenager now routinely depends. So you may want to model and insist on some "when we're talking" rules.

- No conversations with an earplug attached elsewhere.
- No giving half a listen because the other half is watching TV.
- No competing with blaring music that drowns conversation out.
- No talking when the computer or handheld device is actively in play.
- No interruptions of a conversation to check on or answer a cell phone call.

Clear channel communication, where sending and receiving data is unobstructed and undistracted by electronic interference, is best accomplished when all such devices are turned off.

THE NEED TO KNOW

Not only can absence of conversation create loneliness and estrangement between father and teenager, this lack can frustrate a very powerful human need, what I call *the need to know*, to negative effect. What is the need to know? Being social animals, people are information gatherers, when they meet always asking questions like "How are you?" "How have you been?" "What's going on?" Parents vary widely on how much they need to know to feel securely informed but they can never know it all. And come adolescence, as the teenager's life gets more worldly and complex, parents are going to know less about their son or daughter than before.

As a father you are continually gathering information about your adolescent to be up to date and about the teenager's life. There is information about the past: "How was your day?" There is information about the present: "Do you have homework?" There is information about the future: "What are your plans this weekend?" It takes a lot of discussion to satisfy your need to know as a father, to feel adequately informed about the young person's life, for which you bear some responsibility. To appreciate the power of this need, consider what can happen when it is denied.

Suppose your teenager is out of cell phone contact because the battery has died. She was due home from high school band practice at 6:00 P.M. and it's 7:00. Responding to the lateness of the hour, you begin to wonder: "Where is she?" By eight o'clock, and still no word, you become concerned: "Is she okay?" You decide to call a couple of her friends, but they don't know where she is. By nine o'clock you start to worry, asking yourself questions of the "What if?" kind: "Suppose something bad has happened to her?" By ten o'clock, anxiety is ruling your emotional state as you now answer your worries with your fears: "She could have had a car accident or worse!" And just when you are weighing whether to call the police, in walks your daughter, happy to see you, but alarmed by the look on your face. "Is something wrong?"

she asks. "I meant to call, but with all I had to do I forgot." And she explains what kept her busy the last four hours.

Do you greet her with welcome relief? You probably do not. You react to her arrival with anger instead. Why? Because by denying your need to know rather than keeping you adequately informed, she left your ignorance at the mercy of your imagination, and you imagined the worst. What started by you simply wondering ended in your anger and blame. "Here I've been scared for the past two hours that something harmful happened to you! Next time, if you know you're going to be very late, you find a way to give me a call!"

In your relationships with family, to the degree you can, honor everyone's need to know. Ignorance is experienced as the absence of necessary information. It can have powerful emotional consequences when it becomes a staging area for wondering, worry, and fear. It is in the best interests of the relationship that you and your teenager keep each other adequately informed about what you each need to know. And lest you think ignorance is only painful for the father, think again.

Consider the dad who tells his teenager son: "I had to leave work for the doctor's so they could run some tests. I'll let you know the results when I hear." But since he's feeling better and the tests were negative, the man forgets his promise until, in anger, several days later, the boy confronts the man. "Why didn't you tell me? I thought you'd been hiding some bad news!" Guessing games in communication are mostly played by guessing wrong and by creating false assumptions of the fearful kind.

SEX ROLE DIFFERENCES

Staying connected with your teenager, however, can not only be complicated by insufficient dialogue; it can also be affected by sex role differences in communication that can come into play between father and daughter. As Deborah Tannen writes, "I subscribe to a cross-cultural approach to cross-gender conversation by which women and men, boys and girls, can be seen to accomplish and display coherence in conversation in different but equally valid ways." (See Tannen, 1996.)

While all people share conversation about feelings, thoughts, and behaviors to create verbal communication, men and women often share different kinds of information. Male to male conversation tends to include more sharing about behaviors (doings and events) than feelings. Female to female conversation tends to include more sharing about feelings (experience and awareness) than behaviors. And when it comes disagreements, the male tends to argue to win, while the female tends to discuss to understand. In arguments, males commonly complain that women are "irrational" (focused on feelings), while females commonly complain that men are "insensitive" (focused on behaviors). In male/female conflict, the woman often wants to explore the differences at issue to get a deeper sense about what's going on, while the man often wants to rush for closure and win control in order to be right.

"Men and women have been misunderstanding each other for generations ... Numerous research articles and books have been written on the subject, with all of them drawing the same conclusion: Men and women speak different languages. There have been many attempts to explain gender differences in communication with heredity and environment at the top of the list ... In general, men talk to give information or to report. They talk about things ... rather than people. They convey facts, not details. They are goal orientated ... Women, on the other hand, talk to get information and to connect or gain rapport. They talk about feelings rather than things. They convey feelings and details. They are relationship orientated." (See Holmes & Sachs in *Ohio State University Extension Fact Sheet,* HYG–5192–98.)

So here is a common father/teenager daughter confrontation.

Daughter: "You don't understand how I feel, and you don't want to!"
Father: "What I don't understand is you acting this way, and I want it to stop!"

The father is better served delaying his need for closure and control in order to bridge the difference between himself and his daughter, exploiting the conflict as a chance to get better acquainted with her and her emotional world. He could do so by responding differently. "Please tell me what I need to know about your feelings to better understand what's going on."

COMMUNICATION = SPEAKING UP

Communication is about more than sharing three kinds of data. It is a process of speaking up in order to create self-definition—it allows other people to know who and how we are and what we need and want. It is through speaking up about our selves that we become socially outspoken and socially known.

Consider five functions of speaking up (for everyone, not just adolescents). Each function is primarily learned in the most formative classroom of all, the family of origin in which we all grow up. This is the classroom a father helps to create for children and adolescents of his own, a very formative responsibility. With each function, there is a common fear that can make this kind of speaking up hard for adolescents to do.

1. *Speaking up to express.* A primary function of communication is to process experience by talking out what is thought or felt, and by describing the impact of events that have occurred. By this spoken acknowledgment, stresses of daily living can be relieved as they are recognized and shared. "I manage pressure better when I can talk my problems out." *The adolescent fear is:* "If people knew how sensitive and insecure I felt, they might think less of me."

2. *Speaking up to explain.* This function of communication is for declaring needs and points of view. By doing so, wants and beliefs can be understood. "I can let people know why I think the way I do." *The adolescent fear is:* "If I state an opinion, people might disagree with it and then I'd either have to defend it or back down."

3. *Speaking up to question.* This function of communication is for finding out, to understand what's happening. By doing so, the need to be informed is satisfied. "I can ask about what I don't understand." *The adolescent fear is:* "If I ask a question, people will see how I am ignorant and make fun of me for not knowing."

4. *Speaking up to confront.* This function of communication is for taking stands when hurt or wronged. By doing so, oppo-

sition to unacceptable treatment is asserted. "I can use words to set limits and protect myself." *The adolescent fear is:* "If I take a stand to take care of myself, people can just use that stand to attack me even more."

5. *Speaking up to resolve.* This function of communication is to confront and mediate differences. By doing so, conflicts can be settled. "I can work out disagreements." *The adolescent fear is:* "If I agree to fight for what I want and then don't get it, I'll end up losing and even losing face."

It can take courage for the adolescent to speak up, more so with peers than with parents because friends are fickle and not generally as committed to you as parents are. Growing up, most young people do not learn to perform all five functions of speaking up equally well or with equal comfort. In consequence, this variation in outspokenness can limit how adequately they communicate about themselves at home and with peers.

For example, a young man may have learned to resolve differences well, but has a harder time asking for help because this shows a lack of self-sufficiency, even when he could use some direction. A young woman may express her feelings very well, but avoids taking stands for her best interests because she doesn't like to confront others and create discomfort. When a father sees his teenager having difficulty speaking up at home or with friends, he should coach her to develop that skill. He might say: "Every time you back off from disagreement with your boyfriend and let him have his way, you create a relationship on terms he likes and you do not. How could you help yourself to speak up and get more of what you want?"

One way to make discussion of about these complexities okay is for a father to give his teenagers an assessment of himself at their age: "When I was in high school, I didn't express hard feelings very easily because I was afraid of what others would think. So I ended up living under a lot more pressure than I do now that I have learned to be more comfortable talking about problems in my life. I was good at explaining and confronting because I took debate and loved it. I wasn't much for asking for help because I thought that wasn't manly to do. And I shied away from resolving conflicts because in my family people weren't supposed to disagree. I tell you this to say that learning to speak up in different ways can take a lot of practice, some of it scary. But it's worth it, because the more you're known, the more people are likely to treat you how you like."

THE PROBLEM OF SHUTTING UP

But what about the opposite of being socially outspoken? What about a person who is reluctant to declare and reveal themselves, someone who is used to shutting up? While shutting up is important for good listening, it can have a down side when adolescent fears prevent speaking up. One point a father can make clear is that worries about speaking up do not end with adolescence. They are a harsh reality of adult life.

Feel free to talk to your teenager about the hardships of speaking up. For example, it creates exposures that can feel risky when confessing a wrong, expressing a hurt, declaring a want, disclosing a secret, admitting a mistake, confiding a fantasy, breaking a promise, arguing an unpopular point, or being a whistle blower. You can describe many so-called "good reasons" for not speaking up. People may want to avoid trouble, please significant others, or keep everybody happy. Yet by shutting up, they pay a price. They sacrifice having their feelings, thoughts, beliefs, and preferences truly known.

One father shared from his own sad experience of shutting up. "Just to fit in, I laughed with everybody else at a hate joke told at the office when I really didn't think it was funny. I wish I had said so, but I wasn't brave enough at the time. Now I suppose people at the office assume that kind of prejudice is how I believe. I'll tell you the truth. Speaking up is the work of a lifetime. It never gets easy. But as you make your way in the world, there's probably no skill more important to have."

This is a father who had to learn speaking up the hard way because it was not his birthright. He came out of a family background where children were to be seen and not heard, to be silently obedient, and given to understand that speaking up would be punished as a disrespectful act of talking back. In this oppressive family, he learned the skills of shutting up.

- Instead of *expressing,* he learned to be silent and keep his experience to himself.
- Instead of *explaining,* he learned to keep his opinions to himself, deferring to authoritative others.
- Instead of *questioning,* he learned to live with anxious ignorance, waiting to be told or not as others pleased.
- Instead of *confronting,* he dared take no stands when he felt hurt or wronged, accepting any treatment given.
- Instead of *resolving,* he withdrew from differences, avoiding conflict at all costs because it felt unsafe.

Only through marrying a woman who spoke up when there was something hard to say, and who expected this forthright communication in return, did this man learn the skills he is now encouraging in his children. With the support of his wife, he helped create a family different from the one in which he was raised, one in which children and adolescents felt safe to speak up, with no fear of put downs or punishment.

Because of relationship training and parental commitment, when it comes to discussing hard issues with teenagers, confronting them on what they would rather ignore, mothers are often more comfortable speaking up than fathers, who may tend to let such issues go.

ENCOURAGING WAYS TO SPEAK UP

To encourage communication, there are three simple steps a father can take:

1. *Model speaking up.* Routinely talk about your thoughts and feelings and events in your day, and you encourage children to do the same for themselves.
2. *Support speaking up.* Take the time to pay attention to speaking up by listening with interest, and you encourage children to value being known.
3. *Keep speaking up safe.* Refrain from criticism, ridicule, or sarcasm in response to their communication, and you encourage children to have no fear of speaking up.

Of course, children must be taught some guidelines for speaking up. They need to be taught not to dominate all communication, to be willing to "share the stage," for example, as some eldest or only children are loathe to do. And they must be taught not to use words for abusive effect, with impulsive or calculated intent to hurt, for example, as some willful children are prone to do.

SHYNESS AND SHUTTING UP

A father cannot force communication from the young person, but he can explain how shutting up can lead to the painful state of being left alone. He can explain to his shy and lonely 12-year-old some consequences that being quiet and non-communicative can create.

- "If you don't *express* your emotions, then people can't know what's going on inside you, so they may act unmindfully of how you feel."
- "If you don't *explain* your point of view, than people can't know what you think, and so may assume you have no strong opinion either way."
- "If you don't *ask,* then people can't know what you need to know, and so may not be able to give you information you need to understand."
- "If you don't *confront* people when you feel they are not treating you fairly or right, then they can't know when their actions are offensive, and so may not change what you wish they would correct."
- "If you don't *disagree* with people over some difference between you, then they can't know what you each want is in conflict, and so may not be able to work out the issue you would like resolved."
- "If you don't speak up and let yourself be known, you may be misunderstood. Other people might conclude that you're acting snobby by refusing to talk with them, thinking you are shutting up because you feel superior, not because you are shy."
- "There's nothing wrong with being shy. Just don't let feeling shy determine how you act. By acting shy, feeling shy gets worse."

After another teenage argument and being told more than you want to hear, you may wonder if having a socially compliant child is to be preferred to an outspoken one, but in the long run it is not. Later on in life speaking up will serve that young adult better than shutting up. When it comes to getting along with others, effectively making one's way in the world, and ensuring good treatment to support self-esteem, speaking up is extremely important.

WHEN YOUR TEENAGER WON'T TALK WITH YOU

Suppose your teenager deliberately shuts up to keep you out of his life. Sometimes a father, angry at feeling dismissed, will let emotions rule his response, thereby encouraging his silent teenager to close up more. "Nothing makes me madder than when you won't talk with me!" storms the father. Now the man has inadvertently just given the teenager a key to his dad's emotional control. "Not talking to my dad can really get him upset!" There must be a better way to handle non-communication, and there is.

What if your teenage son just freezes you out? What if he treats his life as none of your business? What if he refuses to answer your questions or tell you what's going on? While your son's tactic and your feelings are both understandable, there is in fact something you can do to change the dynamic.

First understand that your son's tactic, which is a time-honored one, is based on the assumption that parents are best kept in the dark. The less they are told the better. So, in service of more independence, your son is keeping you in ignorance to keep you out of his life. Feeling kept out, you feel more frustrated in response.

What can you do? The answer is to hold your son responsible for the consequences of not talking. To do so, begin by declaring something like this. "Whether you choose to talk to me is entirely up to you. I am not in the business of forcing communication. However, you do need to know that in the absence of any information from you, and feeling disconnected on that account, I will have to manage my ignorance my own way. I will have to use my own imagination to come up with an explanation for what may be going on in your life, and based on that understanding (or misunderstanding) I will then make a decision about what is best for me to do. For example, I may suppose from your not talking to me that you have something serious to hide, and in consequence I may decide to impose some social limits on your freedom and reduce the money we provide to protect you from possible harm. Of course, you may find my thinking off base, my conclusions unwarranted, and my actions inappropriate. But when you refuse to communicate with me you give up the power to accurately inform my understanding and effectively influence my decisions. But as I said at the beginning, whether or not you talk with me is always entirely up to you."

Make speaking up safe and rewarding to do. Coach your teenagers. If your teenager decides to shut you out by not speaking up, then inform that young person that there are consequences.

A FATHER'S RESPONSIBILITY

A father will not get his parenting job done by shutting up (except when he holds back discouraging or damaging words that do more harm than good, or is making an effort to listen). A father's job is to continually speak up to his teenagers, providing a clear value structure for responsible conduct. He speaks up to express appreciation when they choose to live within such conduct ("Good for you for refusing to join in the vandalizing"). He speaks up and confronts them when they do not ("Posting that kind of personal information about yourself on the Internet can attract dangerous attention and creates a reputation you will now have to live with").

A father's job is to provide an ongoing sense of reference so his teenagers can always say: "I know where my dad stands even when I don't like listening to what he has to say. Even when I don't agree with it, I know he cares when he tells me what he believes is right and what is not." By speaking up, a father is doing everything he can to provide a reference for how to act and to inform his teenagers' choices.

"Speaking up" is like public broadcasting. Think of it this way. Every day your teenagers are listening to a multitude of stations, all competing for their attention, all striving for influence—from actual media outlets, to popular music, gossip, and peer persuasion. A father's job is to provide a home station that is on 24 hours a day, that keeps sending a constant message about love and responsibility that his teenagers may sometimes tune out but can never turn off. In general, the best fathers never shut up, except when listening to what their teenagers have to say. So, stay on the air and keep broadcasting: "This is K-DAD 101, your friendly fathering station, here to remind you about what can happen in life, and here to inform you about how to live your life so that it works out well."

CHAPTER ELEVEN

FATHERING A TEENAGE DAUGHTER

ttention: If you have a teenage son, this chapter about fathering a teenage daughter will still be of help. So read on.

Adolescence is a period of separation and differentiation when issues of primary attachment and sexual similarity to parents assume more developmental importance. These two issues can create special challenges for a father with his adolescent daughter. Her growth toward independence in adolescence plays out according to two major conflicts with him: *attachment versus separation,* and *similarity versus differentiation.*

- During *separation,* she wants more freedom from his restraint, wants more time with friends than with family, and wants more privacy and less of his supervision. The common separation complaint to her father is: "You never let me do anything!"
- During *differentiation,* she declares, through words and actions, that she is different now than she was as a child, that she wants to be treated differently than she was, is different from parents, and will be different from how they want her to be. The common differentiation complaint to her father is: "You don't understand me!"

She must separate from him during adolescence to claim independence (wanting more time apart) and must differentiate to claim individuality (wanting to act older). Both conflicts can create a crisis of disconnection for a father.

In counseling, I've had dads complain that they don't know how to be as close with their daughters now that they've become adolescents. The daughter doesn't have much to say to her father any more. She's out of the house, closeted in her room, on the phone or computer, or spending time with friends. Her father feels cut out of the loop. Even worse, she may tell him she has nothing in common with him anymore and that he's boring to be with. In frustration, a father can wonder: "What am I supposed to do, just leave her alone?" The answer, of course, is "no." Insist on parent time and family time with her. Remember: Friends come and go, but family is forever. You will continue to love her no matter what, but where, for example, is she left when her best friend takes her boyfriend? Don't allow her focus on peers to obscure her deeper attachment to parents that she is too socially preoccupied to attend to. Instead, keep initiating regular times and special times to be together.

WHY AN ADOLESCENT DAUGHTER CAN PERPLEX A FATHER

Come adolescence, boys and girls separate from childhood, forsake the primary company of parents for the preferred companionship of peers, and begin the journey toward young manhood and young womanhood. While the child wants to remain a child, the adolescent wants to become an adult, and not just a generic adult, but one with specific sex role characteristics.

Parents provide the basis for gender definition during the adolescent's childhood. "A child's earliest exposure to what it means to be male or female comes from parents. . . . Many studies have shown parents treat sons and daughters differently. . . . The parent-child relationship has effects on development that last well into adulthood." (See Witt, in *Adolescence,* summer 1997.)

With the increased awareness of oneself as "young man" or "young woman," the adolescent is increasingly concerned with gender questions.

In consequence, the gender definition of each parent becomes more salient than ever before—mom as one model of woman, dad as one model of man. There are identity questions and there are expectation questions to be answered for both son and daughter. The gender identity question for the daughter is, "What kind of woman is my mother, and is that the kind of woman I want to be?" The gender expectation question is, "What kind of woman does my father treat me as and value, and is that the definition that I want to fit?" All the while, of course, the adolescent is also consulting the world of peers, of fashion, and of media entertainment for idealized models to follow and sex role images to fit.

How do you know when your daughter has entered adolescence?

> Parents know all too well that something is happening to their daughters. Calm and considerate daughters grow moody, demanding and distant. Girls who loved to talk become sullen and secretive. Girls who liked to hug now bristle when touched. Mothers complain that they can do nothing right in the eyes of their daughters. Involved fathers bemoan their sudden banishment from their daughters' lives. But few parents realize how universal their experiences are. Their daughters are entering a new land, a dangerous place that parents can scarcely comprehend. Just when they most need a home base, they cut themselves loose without radio communications.... Parents experience an enormous loss when their girls enter this new land.... In place of their lively, affectionate daughters they have changelings—new girls who are sadder, angrier and more complicated. Everyone is grieving. (See Pipher, 1994.)

WHEN AN ADOLESCENT IS GAY

For the father, the onset of adolescent change requires the utmost understanding and sensitivity toward his daughter's sex role and gender development. One common, albeit small, variation of this development, one that a daughter usually keeps to herself during early adolescence, is the dawning awareness that she is gay. When a daughter (or a son) comes out to parents, usually in the later teenage years or early twenties, it is not just parental understanding that is needed, but parental acceptance. It may prove a more difficult adjustment for a father to have a gay son than to have a gay daughter because in the son the dad not only sees his own reflection, but also feels responsible for how his son turns out to be as a man.

By the time your daughter has attained enough self-acceptance to make this disclosure, she has already traveled an arduous emotional path that you probably were told nothing about. "Coming out" refers to coming "out of the closet," a phrase that means coming out of hiding, which is what most young people do when they are starting to come to terms with their homosexuality. "For children growing up gay almost always include[s] periods of black despair and suicidal thoughts. In fact, gay teenagers do commit suicide in disproportionately high numbers and legions of them self-destruct through substance abuse and promiscuity." (See Bernstein, 1999.) Should your adolescent daughter (or son) become despondent, report thinking about suicide, act suicidal, or get into substance abuse or sexual promiscuity, in the course of getting help for your teenager, make sure the helper is attentive to possible struggles with sexuality.

When I counsel families in which an older adolescent has just come out, parents always seem to focus on this question: "What difference does this really make in our relationship with our child?" From what I have seen, even acceptance that is initially denied is usually ultimately given. The time it takes for parents to reach acceptance depends on the degree of psychological adjustment that is required. Bernstein (1999) describes the challenge well:

> Guilt is just one of a range of inner torments a child's coming out may arouse in parents. Many parents pass through a process quite similar to mourning the loss of a family member. In fact, they do experience a type of death—that of a set of important images and expectations, including visions of grandchildren and of a respectable and respected future for their child. In the shock of the parents' first reaction, the child of their cherished dreams seems no longer to exist. Healing, as after an actual death, proceeds at different paces for different people, and is marked by disbelief, denial, grief, and anger, and [ends], for most, in acceptance.

So while you are being sensitive and accepting of your child, be sensitive and accepting of your own emotions as well.

BRIDGING THE GENDER GAP

In the first chapter of this book, I describe early attachment differences of mothers and fathers. The mother, by bearing, birthing, and breast feeding, becomes closely, relationally bonded to the infant in ways the father can never imitate. The closeness of the maternal connection to the daughter is made even closer still because of the sexual similarity the mother and daughter share. The sexually similar parent is the one who typically exerts most modeling power for the aspiring young man or young woman. This does not mean that in some ways a son will not want to take after his mother, and a daughter will not want to take after her father. However, the father models manhood for the son, who mostly identifies with his dad, and the mother models womanhood for the daughter, who mostly identifies with her mom. *The closer this identity connection between parent and child from gender similarity, the more extreme contrast and intense conflict may occur when the time for adolescent differentiation arrives.*

Sexual similarity and modeling tend to bond father and son, and common understanding can be encouraged much more easily than between father and daughter, who do not share that similarity. The father has been shaped by gender definitions that have taught him how to be a man, just as the daughter is being shaped by gender definitions that are teaching her how to be female. The father has no experience being a woman, and the daughter has no experience being a man. Added to the lack of primary attachment, this sexual dissimilarity can create a gender gap that only creates more distance between father and teenage daughter, unless they can find ways to bridge the sex role differences between them.

One very effective way I've seen fathers bridge these differences is by identifying and appreciating the human similarity between themselves and their daughters: "My daughter is just like I was at this age and in many ways still am now. When I look at her, I see a lot of myself. Same temperament—we're both extremely intense. Same personality—we're both very strong willed. Same level of motivation—we're both highly ambitious." A father can mine this similarity connection for the influence and instruction it can enable. He can say something like this to his daughter. "You know, you remind me of myself. The way I was and how I still am. Like you, whatever I want I want very much, driving me to achieve the goals I set. Good in some ways, this creates two difficulties for me. Sometimes I run over people to get what I want and I hurt, even lose, valuable friendships in the bargain. And when I fail to get what I want, I get very disappointed and angry at being denied, creating a lot of unhappiness for myself. I tell you this, because although I value my ambition, I've had to learn to use it to work for me, and not against me. Sometimes I think the same is true for you." By reflecting on their shared human similarity, the man can create understanding and perhaps warn his daughter away from the errors of his ways. More important, he can forge a very strong parental connection. "Dad and I are a lot alike."

If you feel more perplexed about how to stay connected to your adolescent daughter, remember that you can learn from women around you. Your wife, sisters, mother, female friends, and most important your daughter have much to teach you if you show the interest and make the effort to listen.

One mother had a helpful idea for her husband when their daughter entered middle school and the girl's changes caused the dad to feel distant from her. "Take over the driving time with her—ferrying her around, dropping her off, picking her up. Driving time can be good talking time." And it was, because through providing this service, he established additional presence in her life, giving them a chance to be together with no particular agenda to discuss, freeing them up to just enjoy each other's casual company. By offering or agreeing to do serviceable activities with her, your relationship relaxes because she decides how she wants you to be involved: as her exercise or practice partner, her shopping companion, her research assistant, or her homework helper, for example. Rather than resent being used, appreciate how you are being of use.

A DAUGHTER'S ADOLESCENT PASSAGE IN THE FAMILY

To achieve independence, both adolescent son and daughter have to separate from parents to socially establish more freedom, and have to differentiate from parents to psychologically establish more individuality. In this process, the daughter often has the hardest time.

Although both son and daughter have to separate from attachment to the mother, that attachment tends to be closer and more intense for the daughter because she is also bound by sexual similarity with her mom. In this sense, the daughter has a double connection—biological attachment and sexual similarity—that she must break. This is why there can be so much conflict with her mother—to create the needed contrast so separation can occur. The daughter's question of her mother during adolescence is: *"Can I be sexually similar to you and remain connected to you, but still become different and independent from you?"*

> In Western culture, mother-daughter tensions spring from the daughter's attempt to become an adult, to be an individual different from and not dependent on her mother.... To have a self, daughters must reject part of their mothers. Always mothers and daughters must struggle with distance—too close and there is engulfment, too distant and there is abandonment.... Mothers are more likely to have the most difficult time with adolescent girls. Daughters provoke arguments as a way of connecting and disconnecting at the same time.... They struggle with their love for their mothers and their desire to be different from their mothers. (See Pipher, 1994.)

Sometimes a father will criticize his wife for getting into so much conflict with their teenage daughter, particularly when he gets into it much less. "Why can't you just try to get along?" he asks, because he doesn't like living around what he has come to refer to as a "mother/daughter battle zone." "The only time you talk is when you fight!" he charges his wife. To which the woman responds, "And to avoid a fight you never talk to her at all!" Both parents are right, of course. The daughter is fighting for her independent life and individual identity with her mother, who is honoring this need by staying in hard communication during an emotionally intense time. The father, by avoiding conflict, avoids connecting with his daughter because he finds this kind of communication uncomfortable. To connect with his daughter, who is often in high conflict mode, he can work with her complaint, not against it, inviting more discussion by listening. Instead of confronting her in disagreement, he can calmly and patiently request, "Please tell me more about what I don't understand, I want to hear." It's hard to argue with a father who sincerely wants to comprehend.

Because there is no history of biological attachment, as there is with her mother, the daughter's sense of distance from her father can be amplified by the sexual difference between them. She has a double disconnection (lack of biological attachment and sexual dissimilarity) to overcome. The daughter's question of her father during adolescence is: *"Can I be accepted by you and connected to you even though I am sexually different from you?"*

> In my study, the majority of fathers fell in the distant relationship category. They may have wanted relationships, but they didn't have the skills. . . . Distant fathers were generally perceived as more rigid than mothers, less understanding and less willing to listen. . . . These distant fathers were often well-meaning but inept. They were likely to work long hours outside the home and have less time and energy for the hard work of connecting with adolescents. Distant fathers didn't know how to stay emotionally involved with their complicated teenage daughters. They hadn't learned to maneuver the intricacies of relationships with empathy, flexibility, patience and negotiation. They had counted on women to do this for them. Some fathers had more than a skill or time deficit. Because of their socialization to the male role, they did not value the qualities necessary to stay in a close long-term relationship. They labeled nurturing and empathizing as wimpy behavior and related to their daughters in cold, mechanical ways. (See Pipher, 1994.)

Your adolescent daughter's passage in the family can be marked by more intense conflict with her mother and by more pronounced distance from you. *Your job is to approach your own conflict with your daughter as an opportunity to better understand her, and to maintain communication with her so that estrangement between you does not occur.*

GIVING YOUR DAUGHTER SUFFICIENT DISTANCE

One objective of adolescents is to put parents at a sufficient social distance so independence can be claimed and relationships with peers can be given the priority they demand. While estrangement from the father can be a source of unhappiness to an adolescent daughter, this pain is preferable to the extreme alternative, an unhealthy intimacy with a father who has become too important, whom she won't let go. If her heart forever "belongs to daddy," how is the young woman ever going to be able to lovingly commit to a life partner?

Unhealthy closeness can take many forms, one of which is that the daughter shines brighter than her mom does in the dad's eyes. If her dad thinks his teenage daughter is praiseworthy in every way, it's not hard to understand his wife's jealousy of this rival for her husband's admiration. It's not hard to understand the woman's insecurity with her husband and hostility toward their daughter. When the mother feels she must compete for the father's attention You need to be sensitive to this by making a clear distinction between the two very different places each woman holds in your life. Parental love for your daughter is not the same as partner love for your wife. You have nurturing love for your daughter, but you have loving intimacy with your wife.

Part of a daughter's job in adolescence is to break away and distance herself from the idolized man of her childhood who mattered so much, and for the father to accept this demotion from primary male in her life to one of secondary importance. Often this change becomes a reality when your teenage daughter becomes sexually active or falls in love. Now her loss of sexual innocence or her romantic infatuation with another person means that your role has changed because her primary attachment to you has been set aside. You must accept that she now puts you at a distance. It is no different from what needs to happen between mother and adolescent son. After all, if she can't gracefully cede her role as primary woman in the life of her son, what kind of mother-in-law is she later likely to be? If the father can't step aside, what kind of father-in-law is he likely to be? Whether married or divorced, straight or gay, as a father you must accept at some time being pushed aside to make room for a primary partner in her life.

Then, of course, damage is done when a father gets incestuously close, using looks or words or touch that cross the sexual boundary, leaving his daughter with a legacy of violation and distrust. As your teenage daughter becomes more womanly, become more respectful in what you say and how you act. Create a safe male presence, not a sexually uncomfortable, embarrassing, threatening, or predatory one. Honor the young woman your daughter is becoming and the increased modesty and sexual privacy she needs; and *never* respond to her or in any way treat her as a woman of sexual interest.

Finally, there is the dad whose anger is dangerous to be around. His rage may prompt him to say hurtful things or to commit hurtful actions. *This is not a distant father. This is an abusive father who is threateningly close.* Dangerous fathers of this kind can leave a young woman distrustful of anger in other relationships for the verbal or physical violence it may portend. This fear can cause her to avoid offense or to placate displeasure to keep a partner's anger at bay. Unhappily, by dancing around anger in future relationships she can recreate a sense of danger where it need not be, fearing any expression of irritation in a male partner as a portent of abuse. In a healthy family, a dad can tell his daughter, "If you ever are anxious around my anger, please tell me and I will manage or express it in a safer way."

AVOIDING EXCESSIVE DISTANCE FROM YOUR DAUGHTER

There is a world of difference between the necessary distance that a daughter exercises during adolescence, and the disconnect that results when a father is unnecessarily distant. It is the father's challenge to understand and manage this distinction so he can give his daughter the safe separation that is required, while maintaining the salient male presence with which she can feel securely connected.

When and when not to be distant from your teenage daughter is an extremely complicated parenting problem. The best most men can do is to get it right some of the time. There are times when your daughter finds you overbearing, and times when she misses closeness with you. You must accept that most grown-up daughters have some complaints about how their fathers handled this delicate issue.

The biggest problem with distance from the father is how it can communicate devaluing and disinterest to his daughter. For example, hear what a high school junior has to say. "I'm a friend person. Relationships mean everything to me. They always have. Hanging out with girl-friends just talking about our lives is one of my favorite things to do. This strikes my father as a waste of time. Where's my ambition? What am I accomplishing? Why don't I *do* something with my life? Dad's got no problems understanding my brother because my brother is just like my dad, living life like it was a game about getting ahead. I'm sure he loves me, but he doesn't value me very much. He doesn't take me seriously. Sometimes I think he kind of writes me off." *For a father to stay connected with his teenage daughter, he must honor and respect her.*

A father who is unable or unwilling to value his teenage daughter when her life becomes focused on relationships with women friends can create distance between her and himself. The risk here is that the daughter will experience her dad's inability to relate to her conduct as disapproval, or worse, believe she is not worthy of serious attention. At worst, she can end up feeling like a second-class child when compared with her brothers, with whom her dad claims gender similarity. It's a powerful law of family life. How a child is treated by her parents influences how that child comes to treat herself. *If you do not take your daughter seriously, she is less likely to take herself seriously.*

More extreme than not being taken seriously is outright dismissal, which occurs when a father finds no grounds for interest in his daughter as she journeys through her teenage years. In counseling, young women describe a change in their relationships with their fathers once adolescence begins. Too old to be treated as his adorable and adoring little girl, the father seems to pull away and have less to do with his daughter. Consequently, when it comes to mattering to men and to finding men who matter, she is on her own, often seeking personal affirmation in male relationships to make up for what her dad no longer gives.

THE ABSENT FATHER

Having a physically, emotionally, or socially absent father can harm a teenage girl. Absent fathers create daughters who feel abandoned; and since most abandonment is experienced as some degree of rejection, the young woman can to some degree reject herself. Lacking approval from her father, she may be unable to approve of herself and inclined to let other people determine how best she should be defined and for what she should be valued.

Without the salient male presence of her father to depend upon as a constant source of caring and communication in her life, the abandoned daughter can end up looking for positive influence in the wrong places. She can reach out to immature male peers or to older men who are ready to exploit her unmet need. She may even continually place herself at inequitable sexual disadvantage, trying to compensate for missing validation by doing what she can to please other men, even if it is harmful to herself.

When men disappear or diminish their family presence during the adolescent years, a teenage daughter can be deprived of important male models. A father is responsible for five major role contributions to his daughter's life.

- He defines how men should be expected to treat her and, how she should be expected to treat men.
- His relationship with the other parent provides the primary model of a man's partner role.
- His respect and esteem for her teaches her much about respecting and valuing herself.
- His authoritative communication about what is wise, appropriate, and right, and what is not, provides her with a reference for personal conduct.
- His consistent guardianship gives her a sense of appropriate security.

For example, a high school freshman girl falls in love with a senior guy's flattering attentions until she awakens to discover it wasn't really love at all and breaks it off. The young man, deeply hurt by the rejection, becomes aggressive, turning pain into anger to hurt her the way she hurt him. So he starts circulating slanderous rumors about her, vandalizes her locker, even makes threatening phone calls to her, stating that he'll make her sorry for humiliating him.

Seeing a bad situation building, in his role of guardian, the father talks to four parties to set restraints on the young man's behavior and perhaps get him help. The father talks to his daughter about not giving any double messages to the young man that would indicate she wants the relationship to resume. He talks to the young man to declare that threats to his daughter must stop. He talks to the young man's parents to get their cooperation. He talks with the school counselor and administration to see if someone there can help the young man with his pain. Of course, if all these interventions do not seem to help the situation, he goes to the police.

Male violence as reprisal for rejection and loss of control is an unhappy reality of adolescent love. If your daughter breaks off a love relationship, keep an eye out for how her former love interest responds. In most cases, there is no reprisal, but in some there is, and you do not want your daughter getting hurt.

PRACTICING THE ART OF APPROACHABILITY

If fathers accept that they are usually at a built-in disadvantage when it comes to maintaining close connections with their daughters during adolescence, they can practice a strategy of communication that can reduce the tendency toward separation. They can practice the art of approachability. This requires creating a receptivity that can encourage their daughters to talk with them, and not dismiss them as too formidable, disinterested, uncaring, or out of reach.

To create receptivity:

- Be immediately available for communication.
- Listen without interrupting or continuing to do something else.
- Maintain eye contact to show you are paying attention.
- Face her (do not stand sideways and look away).
- Repeat some of what you hear to show you're following what is said.
- Express awareness and concern for feelings you hear.
- Express appreciation for being told.
- Take turns talking.
- Ask for help to better understand.
- Listen as long as she has something to say.

Unless she is specifically asking you to help solve the problem she is describing, *just listen.* And when you are listening, be prepared for your teenage daughter to occasionally get frustrated with you and complain: "You're not listening to me!" Should this response occur, ask her, "What am I doing or not doing that causes you to believe I am not listening? I need to know." Sometimes there are physical behaviors you can change to create the appearance of more receptivity (stopping what else you are doing, facing her, making eye contact).

Often, however, adolescents misunderstand what listening is. If you ask her how you are not listening and you hear the three following complaints, take the time to clarify what listening really is. The complaints are:

"You don't understand what I say!"
"You don't agree with what I say!"
"You won't do what I say!"

Explain that listening has to with your attending to what she has to say well enough to be able to repeat back to her what she has said. "That I don't understand, agree, or won't comply with what you say doesn't mean I am not listening. I am. If I do not understand what you say, I am willing to be educated about what I am missing. If I am not agreeing with what you say, I am willing to discuss our disagreement. If I am not doing what you say, I am willing to talk more to see if something can be worked out."

If at this point she gets frustrated and declares "There's no point in talking with you if you won't understand, agree, or do what I want," respectfully disagree. "The first purpose of talking to me is to express what's on your mind, and the first purpose of my listening is to pay attention to what you have to say. That's the connection that communication is intended to create. As for the rest, sometimes I'll understand and sometimes I won't. Sometimes I'll agree and sometimes I won't. Sometimes I'll do what you say and sometimes I won't. But I will always take the time to hear whatever you have to say."

TEACHING YOUR DAUGHTER ABOUT RELATIONSHIPS

There is a very powerful instructional role you can play in your daughter's social life as she becomes more seriously involved in romantic relationships, usually in high school. You can give her some guidance about how to determine if a dating or serious relationship is "good." Because you are usually more the performance parent than the relationship parent for her, your daughter may listen closely when you talk about what you usually do not discuss. Coming from her dad, who has her best interests at heart, these guidelines can help your daughter.

You can begin by honoring her interest in having more significant relationships by explaining that people only learn how to create good relationships by engaging in them. Experience is not only the best teacher, it is really the *only* teacher when it comes to learning how to have social companionship, friendship, feelings of attraction, infatuation, even love. There are four questions she can ask herself about any relationship that comes to matter. Tell her she must be able to honestly answer "Yes" to all four for the relationship to be considered good, or at least good enough.

1. *"Do I like how I treat myself in the relationship?"* For example: "Do I give my needs as much importance as the other person's?"
2. *"Do I like how I treat the other person?"* For example: "Do I respect the other person's right to view things differently from me?"
3. *"Do I like how the other person treats me?"* For example: "Do I like how the other person doesn't criticize me when we disagree?"
4. *"Do I like how the other person treats himself (or herself)?"* For example: "Do I like how the other person manages stress during hard times?"

If your daughter is caught up in the emotional intensity and confusion of first love, a father can pose ten additional questions to help her find her way.

1. "Does each person make a continual effort to be as considerate as possible?"
2. "Does each person feel free to speak up about what matters and feel listened to when those concerns are expressed?"
3. "Do both people avoid pushing and threatening to get their way, and do both people feel that the limits they set are respected?"

4. "Is conflict conducted safely, neither person saying or doing anything hurtful in frustration over disagreement?"
5. "Do both parties keep their word, and honor agreements and promises made?"
6. "Can each person trust the other person to tell the truth?"
7. "Is neither party so possessive that the other is expected to give up spending some time apart—alone, with friends, or with family?"
8. "Do both parties manage anger without doing each other verbal or physical harm?"
9. "Is there equality of sharing in the relationship such that neither party does most of the giving or most of the getting?"
10. "Do both parties refrain from putting down each other with criticism, teasing, ridicule, or sarcasm?"

At some time, in the course of experiencing a serious relationship, your daughter may get stuck in a hurtful situation, and this will be very hard for you to see. Like you, she doesn't want the bad to continue, but neither does she want to give up on the good. The reason love is blind is that it is so often deluded by hope—denying or discounting bad things in the expectation that somehow time will change them for the better. So even if some of the ten signs of good treatment are clearly missing, love, and particularly "in love," behavior can bridge their absence with wishful thinking.

Consider the following example. A daughter's boyfriend loses his temper and speaks hurtful words after having promised not to do so. "But he said he was sorry," she explains. "He didn't mean what he said. He was just angry! If I hadn't made him angry, this never would have happened! So it's partly my fault!"

"I think he's responsible for his anger, not you, " suggests her father. "But deciding that is up to you. However, I can tell you this. The best predictor of treatment you can expect is the record of treatment you have received. If you have objected to past treatment, if he has apologized for past treatment and promised not to do it again but the behavior has persisted, then he has voted with his actions. In love relationships, it's not promises that tell the truth, it's performance. Your job is to love yourself well enough so you do not let love for another person (or fear of losing that love) justify accepting mistreatment of any kind."

The reason why some fathers are such effective instructors about relationships for their teenage daughter is because their focus is often on *performance,* on how treatment is conducted. Their advice is practical. It is objective. It focuses on doing. It describes specific behaviors she can identify and be entitled to expect in a healthy relationship.

SEXUAL HARASSMENT AND SEXUAL VIOLENCE

Even more serious is the father's responsibility for discussing a much harder subject with his teenager daughter, the dangerous reality of sexual harassment that is likely to come her way in high school. One working definition of sexual harassment is: *threatening sexual attention targeted at a person through words or actions.*

The American Association of University Women (see www.aauw. org) has issued three survey reports on this problem.

- In 1993, "Hostile Hallways: The AAUW Survey on Sexual Harassment in America's Schools" (grades 8–11) reported, "the research found that 85 percent of the girls and 76 percent of the boys surveyed have experienced sexual harassment. . . . Sexual harassment takes a greater toll on girls: girls who have been harassed are more afraid in school and feel less confident about themselves than boys who have been harassed."
- In 2001, "Hostile Hallways—Bullying, Teasing, and Sexual Harassment in School" reported, "girls are more likely than boys to experience sexual harassment ever (83 percent vs. 79 percent)."
- In 2006, "Drawing the Line: Sexual harassment on Campus" reported that "nearly two-thirds of college students experience sexual harassment at some point during college, including nearly one-third of first year students."

Given the high incidence of sexual harassment and the damage it can do, let your daughter (and your son) know that should this intimidating sexual attention occur, you would like to be told so you can help, or get them help, to talk out how it feels. You also want to help figure out how to stop it from happening again. You can then use this conversation to broach the subject of sexual violence.

According to the survey "Dating Violence against Adolescent Girls"(see Silverman, Raj, Mucci, and Hathaway, in the *Journal of the American Medical Association,* vol. 286, no. 5, August 1, 2001), "Approximately 1 in 5 female students (20.2 % in 1997 and 18.0 % in 1999) reported being physically and/or sexually abused by a dating partner." Add to this the January 2005 *Kaiser Family Foundation Survey on U.S. Teen Sexual Activity* (www.kff.org), which indicated that "nearly one in ten (9%) of 9–12th grade students report having been physically forced to have sexual intercourse when they did not want to at some point. Females (12%) were more likely than males (6%) to report this experience." In addition, "one-quarter of sexually active 9–12th grade students report using alcohol or drugs during their most recent sexual encounter. Males (30%) are more likely than females (21%) to report having done so."

You need to talk with your teenage daughter of dating or party age about the harsh reality of sexual violence because she is at risk. Explaining the frequent connection between sexual activity and substance use can be one helpful way to begin. Tell her that one important protection against sexual violence is sobriety, for her self and for whomever she's with, because alcohol and other substance use reduce normal restraints and impairs your judgment. Under the influence people can become more unpredictable, forceful, and violent. Under the influence, the young man she thought she knew and could trust can become unusually sexually aggressive.

Explain that sexual aggression can take a very destructive form. The man can use aggressive means to gain a sexual end, which is when rape occurs. Rape is when the woman says "no" and the man uses emotional or physical force to get his sexual way. Afterward the woman is left with emotional injuries that can take years to heal. You are saying all this not because you don't want your daughter to date, but because you want her to do so mindfully, keeping herself substance-free on dates and at parties to keep her safe from the possibility of sexual harm. And you want your son to understand that forcing his sexual attention on anyone is not allowed.

BEING FEMALE = BEING A "MINORITY"

A final source of harm to your daughter is social oppression, the individual and institutional majority actions that can mistreat some minority in a personally demeaning, socially disadvantageous, or destructive way. Keep in mind that we are all judged by a host of basic characteristics such as personal appearance, mental functioning, physical disability, level of income, sex, sexual orientation, primary language, age, race, religious beliefs, and more, and your teenagers are no exception. That your child is being discounted, teased, criticized, excluded, threatened, or pushed around by the socially dominant group because of one of these designations only shows the father what may be in store as his teenager grows up. A person who possesses some kind of minority status in a majority-run system

- may find that ruling norms are biased against them,
- may have freedom of opportunity limited by unequal access,
- and may be subject to physical or social threat.

Like it or not, a father must accept and understand that his teenage daughter, being female in a male-dominated society, has minority status, and is at higher risk of bias, unequal access, and mistreatment on this account. Once she enters middle school, where these oppressive dynamics start to become a problem, and high school, where they become significant, you need to be in communication with her about these issues. They affect both her self-esteem and safety. (As will be discussed in the next chapter, sons can also occupy minority status; one male minority characteristic is race.)

There are three agents of social oppression, and you need to understand how each can injure your daughter's self-esteem.

1. Expressions of *prejudice,* usually in the form of negative stereotypes, communicate to the victim that his or her "kind" is inferior, thereby attacking that person's self-evaluation, one component of self-esteem. *The power of prejudice is the poison of self-rejection,* victims coming to believe the social judgment made against them. Thus a gay eighth grader must

usually struggle with her homosexuality because of what a majority heterosexual culture has taught her to believe. Years of witnessing anti-gay beliefs, jokes, and attacks in society at large and in school not only create a need for secrecy, to preserve social safety, but can create some degree of self-rejection to overcome.

2. Acts of *discrimination,* usually in the form of obstruction or exclusion, keep the victim from developing to full potential, thereby limiting their self-development. *The power of discrimination is the denial of opportunity.* Victims are not supported and are given limited choices when it comes to what they are allowed to do. This often plays out in high school athletics, with more opportunities and funding available for male than female sports.

3. Acts of *harassment,* usually in the form of threats or attacks, communicate to the victim a sense of danger, distracting a young person at school from learning in the interests of preserving safety, thereby undermining self-esteem by sacrificing academic performance. The frightening influence of a single incident can be profound. *The power of harassment is intimidation,* causing victims to live on terms of prejudice and discrimination they often dare not confront out of fear of reprisal. Thus young women who are subject to unwelcome male sexual advances at school—sexual comments, name calling, sexual pressure, sexual gestures, threats, even molestation—often endure in silence what the school should not allow. Every secondary school should have a sexual harassment policy in place, and a staff person to whom such violations can be reported. Check on this at your daughter's school and make sure your questions are addressed.

You need to understand how social oppression works if you are to help your teenage daughter should she become a victim of prejudice, discrimination, or harassment—damaging events she is most likely to experience at secondary school. Remember, in a majority-run system, the minority victim often gets blamed ("She was asking for it, the way she was dressed") and the majority perpetrator often gets excused ("He's really a good kid, and after all, boys will be boys").

- Should your daughter fall victim to *male prejudice,* you may need to give *psychological help.* "What those guys are saying about you is *not* about you, it is about them. It is about their ignorance or their desire to be mean." You can also emphasize Eleanor Roosevelt's maxim: "No one can make you feel inferior without your consent."
- Should your daughter fall victim to *male discrimination,* you may need to give *advocacy help.* "Your equal rights are being violated, and (with your consent) I will help you make a case to challenge the unfairness that is going on."
- Should your daughter fall victim to *harassment,* you may need to give *social help.* "With your consent, I will join you in speaking to the appropriate authorities and bring this to an end."

In each case you are saying to your teenage daughter that if she is demeaned, treated unfairly, or threatened because she is a woman, she can come to you to talk about it. It's important that she understands this because if she accepts that sexual harassment is normal and unavoidable then she may be at greater risk for sexual violence later on. Obviously, you cannot protect her in every situation, as there will be times when you may not be there, so you need to encourage her to speak up for herself as well.

Finally, don't give her a double message about prejudice, encouraging her to be all she can be, but then making degrading remarks about women who have achieved positions of prominence out in the world. Don't treat sons preferentially, putting them first in the family or expecting them to do less around the home. And make sure you talk with your teenage sons so those young men are put on notice not to participate in sexually oppressive practices: "I expect you to treat women your own age with the same respect you'd want other men to give your sisters and your mother."

SEXISM IN THE FAMILY: THE PROBLEM OF ODD PARENT OUT

When the father is the lone man in a household of women, having only adolescent daughters, he needs to demand respect. (This discussion equally applies to a mother when she is the lone woman in a household of men, having only adolescent sons.)

When the father is the only male, he is in danger of becoming the *odd parent out*, treated as a minority member in the dominant female culture of the family because he is sexually different from everyone else. At times he can feel outnumbered and overpowered in defining and deciding how family matters should be. In the worst case, a form of female prejudice can develop, equating his being sexually different with having an inferior capacity to understand and relate to his daughters. Then discrimination can keep the father from full participation in parental decision making as he is treated like an outsider, excluded from the loop of information in which everyone else is often included, simply because of his gender. Quotes like, "I'll tell you, Mom, if you promise not to tell Dad" and "Your dad doesn't need to know" may sound familiar.

Based on the prejudice that dictates the father lacks credibility, he is denied information available to everyone else (discriminated against). Based on discrimination that denies him information available to everyone else, the father lacks credibility because of ignorance about family female life (he is prejudiced against). As the father loses credibility from prejudice, wife and daughters share less with him, and as this happens, his role as father becomes marginalized in the family.

The mother is often given more confidence, respect, empathy, authority, and support by the daughters than the father, to whom dismissive comments like, "Oh, you're just being a dad!" become common. Sometimes it feels to the father like he's being loved in spite of his parental designation and not because of it. To be treated as a second-class parent in the family by teenagers and a spouse he loves because he is in the sexual minority can hurt. So what is to be done?

When incidents of sexual prejudice or discrimination, no matter how small, no matter how innocent, are directed at a father in the family, he must assert his equal importance as parent in family affairs. He must not allow himself to be put down or be shut out.

Teenagers who learn same-sex superiority and dominance in the "odd parent out" family are likely to carry those beliefs and behaviors into families of their own. Of more immediate importance, however, is that they are being denied full access to and full benefit of their other parent. When the father allows his equal worth as a person and parent to be discounted, diminished, or demeaned, the whole family loses out. The father loses self-esteem, his spouse loses respect for him, and his teenager daughters lose the contribution of his full influence and participation in their lives.

Here's how one older adolescent describes the loss of her father in her family.

> My father? Once the three of us girls hit our teenage years, he kind of disappeared, still working with Mom to support the family, but mostly leaving us to her unless we got seriously out of line. We still loved him and he still loved us, but now it was more at a distance. Mom started doing most of the parenting because she understood what her daughters were going through when he didn't have clue. It just felt natural to go to her. I remember him being grumpy a lot during our teenage years, not that we wanted to talk with him that much anyway. He kept to himself at home except for time he took with Mom. Looking back, I suppose I missed him in a way, but to tell you the truth, I really don't know what I missed.

A father who is consigned the role of odd parent out in his family misses out on connecting with his teenage daughters who (whether they know it or not at the time) miss out on connecting with him.

To sum this chapter up: If you are fathering a teenage daughter, keep significant closeness and necessary distance; listen when you disagree; ask for help when you don't understand; be sensitive to gender differences and look for human commonality; respect your wife and daughter's need for conflict; support and guide your daughter in creating healthy relationships; be approachable; guard against sexual harassment, sexual violence, and sexual oppression in her life; and don't allow yourself to be marginalized as a parent.

CHAPTER TWELVE

FATHERING A TEENAGE SON

Attention: if you have a teenage daughter, this chapter about fathering a teenage son will still be of help. So read on.

Unlike your teenage daughter, who has a "double disconnection" to bridge with you during adolescence (from lack of original attachment and lack of sexual similarity), your teenage son, because of sexual similarity to you, often has an easier connection to make to you, and you to him. Father and son may mutually identify based on gender commonality, may share male recreations and interests together, and may have a common focus on work performance and accomplishment. And you may share the same approach to communication. You both may be more comfortable talking about interests and happenings than emotions and experience, content to discuss what each is *doing* more than how each is *feeling*. Add up all of this, and it may feel easier to pal around with your teenage son than with your teenage daughter.

This unique connection between father and son can create the appearance, and sometimes the reality, that you value and favor a son over a daughter, who may feel that she is seen as a disappointment, as inferior or second best. This experience of parental favoritism can be harmful. One study about "The relationship between perceived parental favoritism and self-esteem" (see in Sherman & Zervas, *Journal of Genetic*

Psychology, vol. 155, 1994) found that "no-favoritism subjects had higher total self-esteem than the nonfavored subjects." In other words, subjects who felt that there was no parental favoritism expressed in the family felt better about themselves than subjects who felt parents favored other children more.

Furthermore, "Sons have a definite edge as far as parental preference for children is concerned. Most parents prefer male children throughout the world." (See Witt, *Adolescence,* summer 1997.) Sexual favoritism of this kind can be doubly destructive. It can penalize your daughter for being different and increase pressure on your son to be like you, and, as we all know, sons and fathers can be quite different from each other.

While the teenage daughter has an easy time differentiating from her father, but a harder time connecting to him, the teenage son often has an easy time connecting with his father, but a harder time differentiating from his father's definition of what a man should be. This task of differentiation can be complicated by the son's beliefs about measuring up to the man, surpassing what his father has done, or fulfilling what his father always wanted but was never able to accomplish. All three motivations encourage similarity to the man, since imitation, competition, and obligation create resemblance. In each case, the son often pursues the objective of gaining the man's approval by becoming like his father.

In consequence, there are three fears that can plague your adolescent son. These fears are about:

- not doing as you did and earning your criticism;
- doing better than you did and earning your envy or your resentment;
- and not filling your unmet dreams and earning your disappointment.

If in words or actions you give a mixed message, "Do what you like, but follow my way," "Do what I do, but don't outperform me," "Pursue your own goals, but remember my dreams," your son can't win.

Better to make clear that as far as your concerned, between father and son there is no comparison to be made, no competition to be created, and no future compensation to be made. Say to your son: "You are not in this world to copy me, I have no need to do better than you and the only ambitions I want you to satisfy are your own. My joy and my job is to support and encourage the growth of a life that works out well for you."

An adolescent son must assert sufficient individuality and independence to claim his identity and live on his own terms. In doing so, he challenges two similarity demands that you as a father, in your role as parental authority, commonly make. You ask that he:

- Fit into the your framework of acceptable family behavior. "Live within the choices we allow." To which, in words or actions, your teenage son may sometimes respond: "Sometimes the rules I choose to follow will be my own."
- Meet the your performance expectations. "Do as well as I say." To which, in words or actions, the teenage son may sometimes respond: "The goals I set are up to me."

To become his own man, your teenage son must resist and reject total similarity to loosen the connection that binds you. Through this process of contrast and opposition, differentiation, individuality, and independence are claimed. This differentiation is usually of a trial, not terminal, nature. To some degree, your teenage son must rebel against the path you recommend to find his own. In cases where a father tries to force similarity ("You will do as I say!"), or where there is worshipful similarity by a boy ("I want to be just like you!"), the young man may resort to extreme resistance to emancipate himself and become his own person.

So a 17-year-old son, in order to free himself from the bondage of similarity he feels his father is insisting upon, declares to the man that he won't live by the father's educational rules and won't finish high school. Thereupon, the young man moves out of his father's home and in with friends, finding a minimum-wage job to pay his way.

Rather than becoming defensive about the rebellion, the father can choose to treat his son's decision with respect. The man states his understanding that living by family rules and going to school just doesn't work for his son any more, and accepts that the young man has decided to live on his own. Honoring his son's decision and the responsibility for self-support being taken, the father offers to stand by with some financial help should his son ever decide to complete high school and want to pursue further education beyond that. Most important, he makes clear that he wants to stay in regular contact, maybe having a meal together every week or so, if that would work for his son. And that is what they do, getting together on more equitable terms, father and son acting more as friends.

Now fast forward six years and the young man has not only completed a GED to get into a community college, he has transferred into a four-year college from which he is soon to graduate. This did not happen because his dad was pushing his own agenda, but because the son, now on his own, independently decided he wanted to follow this path for himself. This doesn't mean that when the father lets his agenda go, the son will inevitably end up claiming it for himself, but it does mean that by letting go, the father's agenda remains in the play of options from which the son can freely choose.

Most of what you as a father really know about life has been gathered through your own experience, so watch out! Preoccupied with this knowledge, and unable to see beyond it, you can forget how much you do *not* know about the infinity of other life paths. To share your path and preference with your son is one thing; to insist the young man follow them into adulthood is another. *Your job as a father is to support your son in finding a path that fits who and how he is, not what you want him to be.* Your job is to bless your son's way so the young man can truly say to you: "Dad, thank you for letting me make my own life." A father who cannot give this blessing, but "curses" his son's choice of path with disappointment, criticism, or rejection creates a disconnection with the young man that can be very difficult to overcome.

SYSTEM SURVIVAL SKILLS

It is one thing to have your son assert his independence by objecting to your agenda as a father, but another to have him oppose *external* authorities. Serious social trouble can ensue. For example, consider what's at stake when your teenage son challenges the powers that be at school.

Compared to girls, adolescent boys do more aggressive acting out in secondary school. Urban middle school data has shown a disproportionality in school punishment, documenting how "boys engage more frequently in a broad range of disruptive behavior." (See Skiba, Michael, Nardo, and Peterson, in *The Urban Review,* vol. 34, no. 4, December 2002.) This pattern of boys receiving more reprimands than girls is a long-standing one, documented over 20 years ago in elementary school: "Available evidence indicates that teachers do tend to give more negative sanctions to boys than girls." (Stake & Katz, in *American Education Research Journal,* vol. 19, no. 3, fall 1982.) And according to the White House initiative, *Helping America's Youth* (see www.helpingamericasyouth.gov), "In 2004, 12% of males 16–24 were high school dropouts compared with 9% females."

Disproportionate difficulty that boys have coping with the demands and restraints of school continues to this day. "There is no doubt that boys are not faring well in school. From elementary schools to high schools they have lower grades, lower class rank, and fewer honors than girls. They're 50 percent more likely to repeat a grade in elementary school, one-third more likely to drop out of high school, and about six times more likely to be diagnosed with attention deficit and hyperactivity disorder (ADHD). Colleges are similar—if boys get there. Women now constitute the majority of students on college campuses, having passed men in 1982." (See Kimmel, in *Dissent,* Fall 2006.)

All this said, by early and mid-adolescence, some teenage boys can make it a point of male pride to provoke adult authority, particularly anyone who publicly orders them around, at school. Actively or passively the teenager may resist that adult

- by ignoring (silent noncompliance),
- by questioning ("Do I have to?"),
- by complaint ("That's not fair!"),
- by argument ("Tell me why!"),
- by testing ("Make me!"),
- and by opposition ("I won't!").

Surrounded by male friends, with whom social standing counts most, the teenager may elect to buck authority to impress his peers, even using the credential of getting punished to enhance reputation. *Resisting school authority is typically more gender-consistent behavior for teenage boys than for teenage girls, hence the discrepancy in disciplinary referrals and drop out rates.*

Coupled with this need to act more "male" by acting more aggressively is the adolescent issue of independence. At an age when freedom is all important, limiting that freedom to suit the tolerances of home and school is increasingly hard for the adolescent to do. However, a teenage boy will ultimately pay if he can't learn to give up enough personal freedom and make enough effort to get along with the demands of a school system.

For example, the male teenager who won't abide authority and accept limits in middle school is unlikely to get very far in high school, discovering too late an unhappy law of social life. When an individual student does battle with an institutional system, the system usually wins. Many teenagers who have officially "dropped out" have really been pushed out by the school.

Thus, should your teenage son run afoul of the school system by resisting demands or breaking a rule, you need to weigh in, supporting him and the system at the same time. Do *not* double punish, apply sanctions at home for infractions at school. Do *not* criticize your son for misconduct at school. Instead, empathize with your son about the consequences the boy must pay. Use your first concern to respond to your son's feelings, then help him understand how individual choice led to institutional response. You want your son to consider how a different choice might have had a different outcome. Your concern is divided between now and later. *Now* you want him to understand the connection between throwing a book in anger and getting detention. But you also have a concern for *later.*

You want your son to appreciate how organizations like schools can be hard for anyone to live in. Consider, for example, what you might say to your 14-year-old son, who has just been assigned Saturday detention for his most recent incident of acting out in class. You might turn this experience of punishment into a larger talking point. "I'm sorry that you have a Saturday detention to pay. That really puts a damper on your weekend, but it does give you time to think. If you had it to do all over again in that situation, are there different choices that could have kept you out of trouble? I know from my own experience—going to school, being in the military, and holding all kinds of jobs—that working in a system is never easy because there are always frustrations. School, military, jobs, they all expect fitting in, following along, and doing what you're told. And they always have a way to punish individuals who break house rules. So maybe that's what you'll choose to learn. I know it's what I've had to learn. Sometimes to get along I have to go along with requirements I don't agree with, I think don't make sense, I think are unfair. This is just how life seems to be."

What you want your son to learn in school, particularly in middle school, is to become a "C" student by mastering the three C's of getting along:

- *Conform* to institutional practices and routines (so he adheres to the class schedule, for example, as opposed to be being tardy);
- *Comply* with rules and restrictions (so he obeys prohibitions against banned belongings, for example, as opposed to bringing dangerous items to school);
- *Cooperate* with requests from authorities (so he does tasks his teachers assign, for example, as opposed to refusing to do work he doesn't like).

Your son will live and work in various institutional systems all his life. Learning how to successfully operate in a school now can teach him how to navigate other kinds of systems later on, because to a large degree they're all the same. In every one there will be some authorities in charge he may not like, some rules to follow he didn't make, and some demands to meet he doesn't agree with. So do your son a favor: Help him learn the three C's, the system survival skills he will later need to know.

In general, if you are an Afro-American or Latino father, you *must* help your sons and daughters learn these system adjustment skills, since public schools nationwide graduate so few of these minority teenagers compared with their white counterparts. "The national graduation rate for the class of 1998 was 71%. For white students the graduation rate was 78%. For Afro-American students nationwide the graduation rate for the class of 1998 was 56%. For Latino students nationwide the graduation rate was 54%." (See Greene in the *Manhattan Institute for Policy Research report,* 2001.) Minority status makes it harder to make one's way through school.

More specifically, if you are Afro-American, helping your son learn system adjustment skills becomes absolutely essential to his future social survival. Not only must your son learn to cope with his minority status and the three forces of social oppression—prejudice, discrimination, and harassment—mentioned in the last chapter, he must make his way in a society that does not work well for too many young black men. "Even when high school graduates were included, half of black men in their 20's were jobless in 2004, up from 46 percent in 2000. . . . In 1995, 16 percent of black men in their 20's who did not attend college were in jail or prison; by 2004, 21 percent were incarcerated. . . . Many of these men grew up fatherless, and they never had good role models . . . no one around them knows how to navigate the mainstream society." (See Eckholm, "Plight Deepens for Black Men, Studies Warn," in *The New York Times,* March 20, 2006.) Teaching your son these social navigation skills is one part of your job; helping him as a minority man cope with the harsh realities of social oppression without hurting himself is another.

ADJUSTING TO AN ADOLESCENT SON

Just as you help a teenage son adjust to the realities of school life, help yourself adjust to adolescent changes that can be difficult to accept because a major *loss of similarity* has occurred. Now your son is becoming different from the child who was content to fit into family and wanted to be just like his father.

Going or gone are the old hallmarks of similarity—predictability, commonality, familiarity, and agreement. In their place, you have an adolescent son who has an interest, or lifestyle, or belief that you find hard to accept. For example, in company with his new skateboarding friends, he sneaks out to run ramps in empty parking garages late one night. This is certainly new and different behavior. But rather than rejecting the person for the practice ("Skaters are just a bunch of trouble makers, and you're not going to be one of them!") you first reinforce family rules against sneaking out. Now he has to stay home next weekend to work the infraction off. Then you can support setting safe boundaries for more risk taking, which in this case goes with this urban sport. You can connect with this adolescent change by accepting his interest with interest of your own. "It's an activity I know nothing about. You find some safer places to practice, and I'll take you there."

In addition to adolescent changes that contrast to how he was as a child, there are also filial changes that contrast to how you are and what you value. So your son may want to quit an activity that you coach or lead, like soccer or Scouts. He may lose interest in what you both have traditionally liked to do together, like going camping and hiking. He may become fascinated by what turns you off, like heavy metal music that you find loudly offensive. He may even reject part of what you stand for, like not caring about school achievement when you are a schoolteacher yourself. To what degree can you accept your son's distancing from childhood and from yourself? Do not engage in a battle between a father who forces similarity for the sake of comfort and a son who insists on diversity for the sake of independence. Your job as father is to keep taking constructive parental stands without feeling like the opposition is personal, accepting your son's push for diversity as a necessary part of the young man's growing up.

BRIDGING THE DIFFERENCES

How can a father treat differentiation in his teenage son so that it is not divisive, so it brings them close and doesn't drive them apart? Treat these differences as bridges to understanding, not barriers to acceptance. There are *differences in want* and there are *differences in involvement,* and you must be able to bridge them both, each in its own way.

Differences in want arise when you forbid an activity your son would like to do. For example, you say: "You can't go to that party because I know it will be unsupervised, older students will be there, and that means the likelihood of alcohol and drugs." Argues his son: "You're overreacting! My friends are going, so their parents think it's okay. You're the only one who doesn't!" Now it's bridge or barrier time. The father can put up a barrier and shut communication down: "I don't want to talk about it anymore!" Or, by turning an opposition point into a talking point, the father can bridge the difference by being open to further discussion. "I'm not going to change my mind, but I am definitely open to hearing about why you think I'm out of step with other parents, what not going will cause you to miss, and anything else you have to say." To accept the role of responsible authority for his teenage son the father must accept that he will more frequently be an obstacle to freedom in the young man's life, a source of frustration on that account. By being a sympathetic and good listener to your son on these occasions, you can create a connection of understanding. You can receive and accept your son's feelings of disappointment at being denied.

At a peaceful time, you can actually lay the groundwork for connecting over future inevitable differences in wants. Do so by explaining something like this: "You need to know that anytime I decide you can't do something you want, and you feel frustrated, disappointed, or angry, I stand ready to hear whatever you have to say. Disagreement over some difference doesn't mean we can't talk about it. In fact, disagreement means we have a lot to talk about because we are seeing the same issue two very different ways. By talking about our disagreement, at least we can understand where we're both coming from. At least we can be together in that. And you need to know something else. I don't enjoy denying you what you want. But I can't just be a yes man for you because that would not be responsible. An unpopular part of my job is looking out for your best interests and saying 'no' when I believe saying 'yes' could get you hurt or in trouble. For what it's worth, I hope you know that I'm not your enemy, I'm your dad. Just because I'm against what you want doesn't mean that I'm against *you*. When I say 'no' it really means I'm on your side."

Bridging *differences in involvement* requires acceptance of another kind. Instead of standing firmly in opposition and listening to your son's complaints, bridging differences in involvement requires the exercise of curiosity and reaching out to be instructed. Instructed in what? Take the time to understand what fascinates and involves your teenager and how it is different from what attracted his attention and enjoyment as a child. It's not just the loss of the common enjoyments that your adolescent son has left behind that leaves you feeling unwanted. New activities and interests that now capture your teenager's attention

may put you off. You may find them unappealing, outlandish, dangerous, or otherwise offensive. Skateboarding? Punk rock, heavy metal,
hip hop, rap? Fantasy computer gaming? Gothic dress and culture?
Body piercings and tattoos? Whatever happened to shooting hoops and
going to football games?

It's important to understand the shift in focus that adolescence
brings to your relationship with your son. A reversal must take place if
you're to stay connected. In childhood your son may have wanted to do
anything you wanted. Although some old mutual enjoyments may
continue into adolescence and even beyond, it is the time for you to
bridge to your son's new world of interests by expressing curiosity.
Learn why he likes the particular activities that hold his interest. You
do this by depending on your son as teacher, guide, tutor, coach, authority, and expert. Become familiar with what challenges and interests
your son, and fresh connections between you are forged. *Now the time
has come for you to sit at the feet of your son and receive instruction about a
new world that you do not know.*

For example, when your 14-year-old wants permission to go to a
rock concert, you might reply: "You can't go . . ." and then be immediately interrupted: "You never let me do anything!" But you might per-
sist: "What I was going to say was, you can't go *unless I come along too.*
I'm interested in learning about what interests you, and it's safer to
have an adult nearby when there's more social risk involved. We don't
need to sit together, but I do want to be around. And I'm curious to
hear that music live."

"Show me," "tell me about," "explain to me," "share with me,"
"teach me," "take me along," are all *bridging statements* helpful in creating connections that span the intergenerational divide created by
the new diversity of adolescent involvements. One of the great gifts
that your children's adolescence can bring you, if you are open to accept it, is exposure to a whole new world very different from the one
in which you grew up. Fathers miss out on this gift in two common
ways. They may fixate and insist on similarity to what they have
known, consigning themselves to the role of disapproving outsider to
their teenager's new and fascinating life. Or, by attempting to shut an
interest down with restriction, they may turn it into a significant
point of conflict.

RESOLVING DIFFERENCES

Conflict is not something you *have* with your teenage son; it is something you *do* with your teenage son. It is a risky performance act, risky because when two men square off over a difference of opinion, if they are not careful it can become a contest over dominance in which harmful means can be used to reach a winning end.

Every time you engage in disagreement with your son you are teaching the younger man (primarily by example in the interaction) how conflict is to be constructively conducted. You are teaching him how to work through and around inevitable differences in values, opinions, perceptions, or wants to reach some imperfect but mutually acceptable resolution. Since conflict creates resemblance (each party is inclined to imitate the other's most influential tactics) you need to model declarative communication you want your son to learn, and not play conflict out on less direct adolescent terms.

Adolescence is a period of manipulation. When it comes to getting freedom from what they don't want to do and freedom for what they do want to do, teenagers can be ruthlessly practical. They seem to have an uncanny ability to know how and when to put the pressure on and when to take it off. Teenagers commonly apply *emotional extortion* pressure on fathers who are often unpracticed and uncomfortable dealing with adolescent intensity.

After argument and evidence have proved ineffective, the teenager often finds that the intense expression of strong emotion, to get what he wants or get out of what he doesn't want, can be persuasive. Here are a few of the more common emotional tactics for a father to beware of, tactics one psychologist (see Narciso, 1975) aptly labeled "get my way techniques."

- *Love.* By acting appreciative, affectionate, and pleasing, a son can soften a father up who is vulnerable to feelings of *approval.* "How can I refuse my teenager when he was so hard to get along with and now he's being so nice?"
- *Anger.* Silently or loudly, by acting offended or wronged, a son can soften a father up who is vulnerable to feelings of *rejection.* "I can't stand it when my teenager acts like he doesn't like me."

- *Criticism.* Acting dissatisfied with the parent, a son can attack the man's character and competence, softening up a father who is vulnerable to feelings of *inadequacy.* "I can't stand being a failure in my son's eyes."
- *Suffering.* Acting hurt and sad, a son can soften a father up who is vulnerable to feelings of *guilt.* "I hate feeling responsible for my child's unhappiness."
- *Helplessness.* Acting like the victim of a parent's decision, a son can communicate hapless resignation and can soften a father up who is vulnerable to feelings of *pity.* "I hate seeing my teenager just give up and act like he's a victim of whatever I say."
- *Apathy.* Acting as if the relationship doesn't matter anymore after some refusal or restriction, the son can communicate a loss of caring that can soften a father up who is vulnerable to fear of *abandonment.* "I don't want to make a decision that might cost my relationship with my teenager."
- *Explosiveness.* Acting as if he is going to lose physical control in response to a parental decision, the child can communicate the possibility, or provide an example, of violence that can soften up a father who is vulnerable to *intimidation.* "I back off and tip toe around when he acts like someone might get hurt!"

To discourage these types of manipulations, you must refuse to play along with the extortion. You must resist the pull of your own emotional vulnerability (to rejection, guilt, intimidation, and the like) and refuse to let it change your decisions. If you give in to this pressure, you may permit freedom you know is unwise, and your teenager may suffer harm from what you reluctantly allow.

The best response to efforts at emotional extortion is for you to model and insist on *declaration.* Manipulation is about tricking or pressuring another person. Declaration is about each person *proposing specific wants* and then *negotiating a specific resolution* that both parties can agree to accept, sometimes with compromise, sometimes with concession. Declaration is about direct communication and generates respect. Manipulation only yields resentment and distrust.

Significant substance use can cause your teenager to become extremely emotionally manipulative in his dealings with you and your

partner. Thus, a teenage substance abuser, bridling at his father's decision to cut off allowance since it could be spent on drugs, and wanting
freedom to use, throws a tantrum by combining anger and suffering
and explosiveness to maximum manipulative effect. In the face of this
emotional onslaught, however, and withstanding his own emotional
vulnerabilities, the father declares: "When you can calmly and specifically tell me *what it is you want* or *do not want to have happen,* I am
happy to discuss my decision with you. But your emotional response is
not going to change my mind."

Any time you are in conflict with your son and he starts using
emotional extortion, call him on it, redirect the disagreement down a
declarative path, and *never resort to emotional extortion yourself.* And
consider the model for conducting conflict you may have been trained
in when competing and sparring with male peers growing up, a model
that your son, with his friends, may well be learning now.

CONDUCTING CONFLICT WITH YOUR TEENAGE SON

A common training model for men in conflict with other men prepares
them to approach disagreement as an opportunity for argument, as a
challenge to self-respect, as a test of dominance, and as a contest to
win. When father and son share this "male" orientation, differences between them can be very hard to peacefully and productively resolve. Instead of discussing their differences to better understand each other
and reach a mutually acceptable resolution, they act as adversaries, each
determined to prevail. The chance to better communicate is sacrificed
to the need for control.

For example, once again your 17-year-old son has violated curfew,
coming home much later than the time you set, partly to show you
that as a high school senior he is determined to set his own schedule.
Once again, you invoke your authority by applying further punishment. You declare: "I'm removing all privileges until further notice!"
And now the battle for control is engaged. "So what?" replies your son.
"With nothing left to take away, how are you going to control me now?
You can't make me and you can't stop me. My life is up to me!" And
now you realize how powerless you are over the one aspect of your son's
life he is determined to control—his freedom of choice. You also realize

how ineffective going toe-to-toe with him has become. You are not going to punish your son into submission. The more controlling you act, the more rebellious he is going to act in response, only imitating your domineering ways. This is when it dawns on you that in a control battle, although you might defeat him this time, he is eventually going to defeat you. His approaching independence makes this final outcome inevitable.

So you decide to switch from a control model for conducting conflict to one that depends on communication, from fighting your disagreement out to trying to talk and work it out. "What I would like to do," you say, "is to start this conversation about curfew over again. I'd like to hear what you need. I'd like you to hear what I need. And then I'd like us to come up with some agreement we can both live with." And that is what you both do, because your son feels better working with you than against you, connecting in a way he has been missing.

As a father, you need to treat conflict as an opening for communication with your teenage son, not a matter of control or power, and this can be very hard to do because power is the ultimate performance issue for many men. *Power is what you can do or not do to get your way, to get what you want.* It can be a matter of taking charge, of dominating a relationship, of mastering a challenge, of winning a competition, of prevailing in a conflict, of being proven right, of having the last word. The more you get your way, the more powerful you can feel.

Conversely, the less you get your way, the less effective and competent you may feel. For some fathers who occupy positions of prominence, power, and respect out in the world, proving inept as an authority at home can feel humiliating. If a teenage son tests his manhood against the manhood of his father by refusing to live up to the man's expectations, it can reduce the man's pride in performance to paternal shame. Unable to tolerate this feeling of performance failure, the father may pull away in apathy or anger: "I don't care what you do with your life, I'm through arguing with you!" Now the son has been given a losing victory. The price of getting his way is the withdrawal of his father.

Sometimes a father will avoid taking healthy stands with his son, will avoid engaging him in conflict about unwise or unacceptable behavior, to avoid overwhelming feelings of performance failure in response to the young man's troubled ways, for which the man feels partly responsible. It may be that substance use the father cannot prevent is causing the son to act in self-defeating or self-destructive ways. Or it may be the father has divorce guilt, believing that by ending the marriage he has set his son on this downward path. In either case, the father prefers to deny what is going on or at least look the other way: "I can't stand to see my son acting this way and I don't want to talk to him about it!"

Why engage in such denial? Because the father is confusing his son's choices with his own, and finds this burden of misplaced responsibility too much to handle. He is blaming himself as a "failure as a father" rather than seeing himself as a father with a son who, at the moment, is choosing to make problematic choices on his own. Of course, if the father declares feelings of misplaced responsibility to the teenager, the young man will exploit the opening that the guilt creates: "That's right, the only reason I'm in so much trouble is because of you!"

What the father needs to do is gather courage. He needs to ask himself questions about feelings that are currently dictating his thinking for him. "What would I choose to do if I were *not* feeling guilty, feeling ashamed, feeling in pain, feeling afraid?" Then the father needs to set these manipulations aside and confront and engage in conflict with his son as he knows a responsible parent should.

POWER STRUGGLES AND POWER TESTS

There are *power struggles* you should avoid with your teenage son, there are *power tests* you should accept, and you must be able to discriminate between the two.

Power struggles have to do with dominance, contesting who is going to be the controlling male. Some "power mad fathers" (fathers who get extremely mad when their power is challenged, frustrated, or proven ineffective) are characterized by a set of traits that can make them extremely oppressive to live with.

The code of dominance that such a man brings to fatherhood can include:

- ruling with rage,
- name calling to humiliate,

- winning at all costs,
- having the last word,
- never apologizing,
- allowing no argument,
- tolerating no refusal,
- admitting no mistakes,
- always being right,
- controlling the family agenda,
- yelling to shut others up,
- being unpredictably explosive,
- bullying the opposition down.

As a teenager, would you feel comfortable disagreeing with a father like this? You probably would not. In fact, come adolescence, you would have learned how to "manage dad" by relying on distrust, distance, and deceit.

Of course the danger of power struggles is that they can escalate into physical conflicts that create immediate hurt and a legacy of harm. As the father, remember that "win now, lose later, and resent always" is the lesson such encounters teach.

Power tests have to do with the teenage son wanting to "go up against his father" to see if he can beat the man in some competition, game, argument, sport, or simply exercise better judgment, proving his father wrong. On these occasions, you need to congratulate your son, acting happy to see him grow: "You beat me fair and square, good for you!" You can even express admiration for your son: "You've gotten better at this than me!"

Growing up for the teenage son often requires cutting the father down from an ideal giant of a man the boy may have worshipped in childhood to an ordinary father to whom the teenage son can relate, one man to another. *Typically it is those fathers who refuse to accept this necessary demotion in their son's eyes, and in their own, who are prone to power struggles to defend superior standing they cannot bear to lose.*

As father, you can actually reduce your son's need to challenge you by deliberately reducing dominance in a number of simple ways. When you do, you alter the relationship between you from being "better than" to being "booster for," recognizing how your son, through experience, understanding, and skill, has achieved competence different from, equal to, or greater than your own. In your relationship, there are numerous ways you can affirm when a new power test has been successful, and they all convey respect for the man your son is becoming:

- You can *ask your son for help with or advice about* something.
- You can simply *compliment your son's performance,* recognizing it as superior to your own.
- You can sincerely *depreciate your own efforts* by honestly, sometimes humorously, comparing them to what your son does better now.
- You can *enter a sport or game competition* with your son and, honestly losing, sincerely congratulate the winner.
- You can *enlist your son as co-worker* on a project in which you two men share equal standing.

Above all, never turn a power test into a power struggle, putting your dominance at stake in a family argument or in a game of competition to prove you are "man of the house" or "the better man." Do so, and whatever victory you gain (or lose) will be at the expense of your connection to your son.

DISCUSSING THE REALITIES OF SEX

In helping your teenage son grow into his maturity, it is important to discuss the *realities of sex.*

Just as you need to talk with your teenage daughter about what constitutes good dating and romantic relationships, you need to talk with your teenage son about the responsible management of sexual activity. But what are you to say? That depends upon your religious persuasion, your values, what you want your son to know, and the guidance you want to provide. What follows is an approach to help you organize your thoughts and feelings on this matter. Take what you like, discard what you don't, and add what works for you. Remember this is not a onetime talk to get over with, but an opening conversation to normalize a continuing discussion of sexual activity, much as in adolescence the discussion of Internet use, of alcohol and drugs, is kept open and ongoing.

Like it or not, as your son grows through adolescence, sexual interest becomes an increasingly central part of his world. The best time to open this discussion is before significant dating and serious relationships begin, certainly by the entry into high school. High school self-report surveys of teenage behavior commonly show that at least half of male and female students report having had sexual intercourse. In January 2005, the *Kaiser Family Foundation* (www.kff.org) *U.S. Teen Sexual Activity Survey* reported: "In 2003, 62 percent of 12th graders had had sexual intercourse compared with 33 percent of 9th graders."

In many cases, mid- and late adolescents view sex partly as a rite of passage into young manhood and young womanhood. It can be seen as certifying that both partners are now adults, although the experience often has different meanings for each of them. While many young women may place sex in a relationship context of caring and being cared for; many young men place sex in a performance context, seeing sex as proof of manliness and conquest.

Here is a beginning script that a father might want to say to his teenage son to add to, alter, or ignore as you see fit:

"Having sex does not prove your prowess if you're a male, it does not prove you're loved if you're a female, and it does not prove that either person has now become an adult. What it does prove is that both are engaging in risky behavior with possible negative consequences. Of course there is the possibility of sexual disease. (When you have sex with someone you have sex with that person's sexual history and most people don't disclose that history because they either don't want to, or they don't know the histories of sexual disease in the partners they have previously had.) HIV/AIDS has to be taken seriously. Being cautious can save your life. As for the 'P' in pregnancy, it also stands for Paternity. When a young woman gets pregnant, the young father has a legally binding financial obligation to support that child for the next 18 years.

"All this said, it is normal and healthy to have sexual energy, sexual interest, and to seek sexual satisfaction. Just remember, however, that you always have a choice. Although I don't want you to become sexually active, if you choose to do so, I want you to *plan* to have sex. When you're sexually aroused with a partner is no good time to decide to have sex because arousal is ruled by impulse. Arousal is satisfaction driven.

Judgment is responsibility driven. At least with planning you can use some protection, which is often missing when sex is just allowed to happen in the magic of the moment. Because planning requires delay of immediate gratification, it also allows you time to consider the impact of having sex.

"Denial is not a form of protection—Just once is okay,' 'It won't happen to me.' Denial promotes sex without thinking. Substance use does the same, freedom from normal care suspending judgment for desire. Many first sexual experiences and 'one night stands' are the result of impaired judgment due to substance use. Drugs or alcohol can also make you more aggressive, less respectful of a woman saying 'no.' Coercion of this kind amounts to rape. When you have sex you need to be prepared to take responsibility for the most problematic outcomes that can occur.

"The problem with casual sex is that there is often insufficient caring involved and care taken so afterward partners can either be at risk for unprotected consequences or feel used. The problem with manipulative sex is that it allows sex to happen under cover of 'love,' one party urging and the other party believing 'having sex shows you love me.' This is not true. As for sex in love, it can intensify a relationship beyond what you may be emotionally ready for.

"All I'm trying to tell you is that having sex is so complicated it is worthwhile to take the time to truly consider not just what you want, but what is wise. Responsible sexual behavior requires exercising good judgment and self-restraint, which I believe is the manly thing to do."

Again, none of the forgoing is what a father has to say, but he needs to weigh in, speak up, connect, and say something. As with substance use, his son's life and happiness could depend upon it. And then there is the matter of money, which is as important to discuss with your teenage daughter as it is with your teenage son.

DISCUSSING THE PRACTICALITIES OF MONEY

By adolescence, what teenagers have and who they are is inextricably linked to money and what money can buy. Possessions and entertainment experiences are a primary way they express and define the person they want to be, and this is as true for your daughter as for your son.

Since early childhood, both have been continually manipulated by a materialistic society to become avid consumers.

Money matters because it is one strand of significant decision making in young life that will only become more challenging and complicated as teenagers grow older. Consider the variety of what people *do* with money, and it becomes a performance issue that you can helpfully discuss. These are some issues that you raise with your son and daughter.

What to do about *being given money?* You might start off by saying: *"Beware gifts of money that come with some obligation for return because they are not as free as they seem."*

What to do about *spending money?* You might start off by saying: *"The law of spending is simply that the more you spend the less you have left, so make sure what you get is worth the loss."*

What to do about *tithing money?* You might start off by saying: *"No matter how little money you have, remember to share with others who are struggling to get by on less."*

What to do about *earning money?* You might start off by saying: *"In addition to providing income, when you can earn money you have some capacity for work someone in the world thinks you are worth paying for."*

What to do about *saving money?* You might start off by saying: *"Saving takes self-control, delaying the impulse for present gratification to finance some benefit or goal you want later on."*

What to do about *borrowing money?* You might start off by saying: *"Repaying borrowed money shows that you keep your word."*

What to do about *budgeting money?* You might start off by saying: *"You will be happier living within your means, on less than you would ideally like, than living beyond your means and feeling the stress of debt."*

What to do about *investing money?* You might start off by saying: *"Investing is always a gamble, taking an actual risk with money for the sake of a possible reward."*

What to do about *credit spending?* You might start off my saying: *"It is easier to buy on credit than to pay off carrying charges that make what you get cost more than it is actually worth."*

What to do about *happiness and money?* You might start off by saying: *"Money can purchase you satisfaction and enjoyment, but it can never buy you contentment or happiness."*

To sum this chapter up: when fathering a teenage son, don't condition approval of him on similarity to yourself; help him learn system survival skills at school; bridge differences in interests with your curiosity; treat conflict as a chance to learn from disagreement; avoid power struggles; affirm power tests; and discuss the realities of sex and the practicalities of money.

A FINAL WORD

The argument of this book is that a father is not a mother, an adolescent is not a child, and fathering a teenage daughter and son require somewhat different understandings and approaches. For a father to remain connected to his children during the normal trials of adolescence, it can be helpful to stay mindful of these distinctions.

Often "the performance parent," a father brings important strengths to his parenting role. With your teenagers, you tend to emphasize such issues as:

- practical reality;
- interests and abilities;
- practice and discipline;
- teamwork;
- ambition and competition;
- effort, goals, and standards;
- achievement and excelling;
- accomplishment;
- working hard now to get ahead later;
- and thinking about and planning for the future.

These are important contributions that many fathers are good at making as a parent. However, they must beware lest this strength turn into a liability. When this performance preoccupation is allowed to rule your role as father, your teenagers are at risk of believing that you only value and esteem them for what they accomplish, not simply for the person they are. Performance is an important part of your teenagers' lives, but it does not encompass the whole individual, which is who you must always keep in mind if you want to be a connected father during their adolescent years.

Finally, remember that fathering a teenage daughter and a teenage son requires a somewhat different understanding, sensitivity, and skill. The challenge in fathering an adolescent daughter is bridging the sex role differences with communication, understanding, and esteem so that estrangement does not cause the daughter to feel devalued, dismissed, or abandoned. You don't want your grown up daughter to look back and say: *"My father never took me seriously as a person because I was his daughter, not his son."*

The challenge in fathering an adolescent son is refraining from criticism and power struggles in an attempt to get the boy to meet the father's expectations, follow his example, or fit his mold. You don't want your grown-up son to look back and say: *"My father treated me as a failure as a son for not becoming the man he wanted me to be."*

As a father, don't discount your teenagers for not being sufficiently similar to you.

THE FATHER'S JOB

What is a father of teenagers supposed to do? Consider some parenting practices that can help your children stay on a healthy course through adolescence, and help you stay well connected to them as they grow.

- Use communication to inform your teenagers' choices and to share about yourself.
- Listen to what your teenagers have to say, let them educate you about their world.
- Help your teenagers learn responsibility from facing consequences of choices made.
- Create healthy rules and expectations for everyone in the family to live by.
- Allow risks from more teenage freedom based on evidence of more responsibility.
- Support the development of teenage interests that become pillars of self-esteem.

- Value conflict as an opportunity to learn more about the differences between you.
- Encourage forming teenage goals that give positive direction to present behavior.
- Treat teenage mistakes as opportunities for education.
- Give a spiritual foundation, however you define it, for your teenagers to rely on.
- Provide your teenagers with your unwavering acceptance, esteem, and love.
- Make and take the time to enjoy your teenagers as they grow.

FURTHER READING

Arnett, Jeffrey Jensen. *Emerging Adulthood: The Winding Road from the Late Teens through the Twenties* (New York: Oxford University Press, 2004).

Bernstein, Robert A. *Straight Parents, Gay Children* (New York: Thunder's Mouth Press, 1999).

Blankenhorn, David. *Fatherless in America—Confronting Our Most Urgent Social Problem* (New York: Harper Perennial, 1996).

Brott, Armin A. *The New Father—A Dad's Guide to the First Year* (New York: Abbeville Press, 1997).

Carter, Betty and McGoldrick, Monica. *The Expanded Family Cycle: Individual, Family, and Social Perspectives (Third Edition)* (Boston: Allyn & Bacon, 2005).

Geary, David C. *Male, Female: The Evolution of Human Sex Differences* (Washington, DC: The American Psychological Association, 1998).

Glennon, Will. *Fathering—Strengthening the Connection with Your Children No Matter Where You Are* (San Francisco: Conari Press, 1995).

Harbin, Thomas J. *Beyond Anger: A Guide for Men* (Berkeley: Marlowe & Company, 2000).

Hutchinson, Earl Ofari. *Black Fatherhood: The Guide to Male Parenting, Reprint Edition* (Los Angeles: Middle Passage Press, 1994).

Mincy, Robert B. *Black Males Left Behind* (Washington DC: Urban Institute Press, 2006).

Narciso, John. *Declare Yourself—Discovering the Me in Relationships* (Upper Saddle River, NJ: Prentice Hall, 1975).

Okimoto, Jean Davies and Stegall, Phyllis Jackson. *Boomerang Kids: How to Live with Adult Children Who Return Home* (Boston: Little Brown, 1987).

Parke, Ross and Brott, Armin. *Throwaway Dads—The Myths and Barriers That Keep Men from Being the Fathers They Want to Be* (Boston: Houghton Mifflin Company, 1999).

Pickhardt, Carl. *Parenting the Teenager* (Austin, TX: self-published, 1983).

Pickhardt, Carl. *Keys to Successful Stepfathering* (Hauppauge, New York: Barron's Educational Series, 1997).

Pickhardt, Carl. *The Everything© Parent's Guide to Positive Discipline* (Avon, MA: Adams Media, 2004).

Pickhardt, Carl. *The Man Who Worshipped Butterflies* (Philadelphia: Xlibris, 2004).

Pickhardt, Carl. *The Everything© Parent's Guide to the Strong-willed Child* (Avon, Massachusetts: Adams Media, 2005).

Pickhardt, Carl. *The Trout King—A Novel about Fathers and Sons* (Philadelphia: Xlibris, 2005).

Pickhardt, Carl. *The Everything© Parent's Guide to Children and Divorce* (Avon, Massachusetts: Adams Media, 2006).

Pipher, Mary. *Reviving Ophelia—Saving the Selves of Adolescent Girls* (New York: Ballantine Books, 1994).

Pollack, William. *Real Boys—Rescuing Our Sons from the Myths of Boyhood* (New York: Random House, 1998).

Rhoads, Steven E. *Taking Sex Differences Seriously* (New York: Encounter Books, 2005).

Smetana, Judith (Editor). *Changing Boundaries of Parental Authority During Adolescence: New Directions for Child & Adolescent Development, No, 108* (Hoboken, NJ: Jossey-Bass, 2005).

Steinberg, Laurence D. & Lerner, Richard M. *Handbook of Adolescent Psychology* (New York: John Wiley & Sons, 2004).

Steinberg, Laurence D. & Levine, Ann. *You & Your Adolescent—A Parent's Guide for Ages 10–20* (New York: Harper & Row, 1990).

Tannen, Deborah. *Gender and Discourse* (New York: Oxford University Press, 1996).

Tannen, Deborah. *You Just Don't Understand: Women and Men in Conversation* (New York: Harper Paperbacks, 2001).

HELPFUL WEBSITES

WWW.CARLPICKHARDT.COM
Parenting articles by psychologist Carl Pickhardt

WWW.FATHERHOOD.ORG
National Fatherhood Initiative

WWW.FATHERS.COM
The National Center for Fathers

WWW.FATHERMAG.COM
Fathering Magazine

WWW.FATHERSDIRECT.COM
The National Information Center on Fatherhood

HELPFUL SUPPORT GROUPS

PARENTS ANONYMOUS
(909) 621–6184
Strengthening families and creating safe homes.

TOUGH LOVE
(215) 348–7090
Support for parents with children having difficulty acting responsibly.

AL ANON
(888) 4AL-ANON
Helping families recover from a family member's problem drinking.

CIRCLE OF PARENTS
(312) 663–3520
Mutual support groups in which parents can help each other.

INDEX

disconnectors and, 151–53
driving time and, 172
electronics and, 154–55
feeling cut off and, 147–51
Internet and, 78–79
maturity and, 99–100
mid-adolescent and, 71–72, 80, 83–86
need to know and, 155–56
psychology of, 146–47
punishment and, 131
responsibility for, 164–65
sex role differences and, 156–57
sexual violence and, 184–85
sons and, 191, 204–6
speaking up and fears of, 158–63
talker vs. listener and, 153–54
trial independence and, 108
uncommunicativeness and, 37, 45, 47,
    147–51, 163–64
competition, 10, 12, 207–8
completion, 98
compliance, 16, 17, 132–33, 197
compliments, 39, 40
compromise, 80
concern, 15, 124–25
conditions, 4, 46–47
confidence, 90, 93, 107, 108
conflict, 15, 17, 20, 25–29, 42
    authority and, 127–28
    concern-based authority and, 124–25
    daughters and, 173–75
    engagement vs. avoidance and, 81–82
    late adolescence and, 91
    lying and, 152
    mid-adolescence and, 79–81, 86
    sons and, 202–6
    trial independence and, 110
    value of, 26–27
conforming, 197
confrontation, 99, 158–59, 161–62
confusion, 81, 103
connecting, as two-way street, 29–30
conscience, 47
consent, 127
consequences, 67–68, 99, 102, 104, 108,
    130–32, 163–64
constructive activities, 68

consultation, 108
contributive authority, 120–21
control, 15, 17, 24–25
    authority and, 124–28, 136–37, 141–42
    late adolescence and, 90
    lying and, 84
    maturity and, 99
    mid-adolescence and, 76
    outside influences and, 134–35
    sons and, 205
cooperating, 30, 122, 197
correction
    criticism vs., 49
    letting go of, 108
courage, 92
courtesy, 39–40
co-worker, son as, 208
credit cards, 45, 103, 109–10, 211
criticism
    by adolescent, 58–59, 152, 203
    of adolescent, 14, 17, 29, 36–39, 49, 50,
        107–8, 111, 122, 152, 196, 213
curfews, 45, 88, 204–5
Current Population Survey (2002), 11

dating, 6, 88, 181–85. *See also* romances; sex
daughters, 5, 78, 167–90
    absent father and, 177–79
    adolescent passage and, 172–74
    anger and, 176
    avoiding excessive distance from, 176–77
    bridging gender gap with, 171–72
    communicating with, 157, 179–81
    criticism and, 14
    father perplexed by, 168–69
    gay, 169–70
    giving sufficient distance, 174–76
    odd parent out and, 188–90
    "respect" and, 17
    romances and, 178–79, 181–83
    sexual harassment and violence and,
        178–79, 182–87
    social oppression and, 185–88
    sons vs., 191–92, 213
    unhealthy closeness, 175
deadlines, 102
debt, 103, 109–10, 211